BURMA'S BRUTAL CAMPAIGN AGAINST THE ROHINGYA

HEARING

BEFORE THE

SUBCOMMITTEE ON ASIA AND THE PACIFIC

OF THE

COMMITTEE ON FOREIGN AFFAIRS
HOUSE OF REPRESENTATIVES

ONE HUNDRED FIFTEENTH CONGRESS

FIRST SESSION

SEPTEMBER 27, 2017

Serial No. 115–72

Printed for the use of the Committee on Foreign Affairs

Available via the World Wide Web: http://www.foreignaffairs.house.gov/ or http://www.gpo.gov/fdsys/

U.S. GOVERNMENT PUBLISHING OFFICE

27–011PDF WASHINGTON : 2017

For sale by the Superintendent of Documents, U.S. Government Publishing Office
Internet: bookstore.gpo.gov   Phone: toll free (866) 512–1800; DC area (202) 512–1800
Fax: (202) 512–2104   Mail: Stop IDCC, Washington, DC 20402–0001

COMMITTEE ON FOREIGN AFFAIRS

EDWARD R. ROYCE, California, *Chairman*

CHRISTOPHER H. SMITH, New Jersey
ILEANA ROS-LEHTINEN, Florida
DANA ROHRABACHER, California
STEVE CHABOT, Ohio
JOE WILSON, South Carolina
MICHAEL T. McCAUL, Texas
TED POE, Texas
DARRELL E. ISSA, California
TOM MARINO, Pennsylvania
JEFF DUNCAN, South Carolina
MO BROOKS, Alabama
PAUL COOK, California
SCOTT PERRY, Pennsylvania
RON DeSANTIS, Florida
MARK MEADOWS, North Carolina
TED S. YOHO, Florida
ADAM KINZINGER, Illinois
LEE M. ZELDIN, New York
DANIEL M. DONOVAN, JR., New York
F. JAMES SENSENBRENNER, JR.,
    Wisconsin
ANN WAGNER, Missouri
BRIAN J. MAST, Florida
FRANCIS ROONEY, Florida
BRIAN K. FITZPATRICK, Pennsylvania
THOMAS A. GARRETT, JR., Virginia

ELIOT L. ENGEL, New York
BRAD SHERMAN, California
GREGORY W. MEEKS, New York
ALBIO SIRES, New Jersey
GERALD E. CONNOLLY, Virginia
THEODORE E. DEUTCH, Florida
KAREN BASS, California
WILLIAM R. KEATING, Massachusetts
DAVID N. CICILLINE, Rhode Island
AMI BERA, California
LOIS FRANKEL, Florida
TULSI GABBARD, Hawaii
JOAQUIN CASTRO, Texas
ROBIN L. KELLY, Illinois
BRENDAN F. BOYLE, Pennsylvania
DINA TITUS, Nevada
NORMA J. TORRES, California
BRADLEY SCOTT SCHNEIDER, Illinois
THOMAS R. SUOZZI, New York
ADRIANO ESPAILLAT, New York
TED LIEU, California

AMY PORTER, *Chief of Staff*   THOMAS SHEEHY, *Staff Director*
JASON STEINBAUM, *Democratic Staff Director*

SUBCOMMITTEE ON ASIA AND THE PACIFIC

TED S. YOHO, Florida, *Chairman*

DANA ROHRABACHER, California
STEVE CHABOT, Ohio
TOM MARINO, Pennsylvania
MO BROOKS, Alabama
SCOTT PERRY, Pennsylvania
ADAM KINZINGER, Illinois
ANN WAGNER, Missouri

BRAD SHERMAN, California
AMI BERA, California
DINA TITUS, Nevada
GERALD E. CONNOLLY, Virginia
THEODORE E. DEUTCH, Florida
TULSI GABBARD, Hawaii

CONTENTS

Page

WITNESSES

LETTERS, STATEMENTS, ETC., SUBMITTED FOR THE HEARING

APPENDIX

BURMA'S BRUTAL CAMPAIGN AGAINST THE ROHINGYA

WEDNESDAY, SEPTEMBER 27, 2017

House of Representatives,
Subcommittee on Asia and the Pacific,
Committee on Foreign Affairs,
Washington, DC.

The subcommittee met, pursuant to notice, at 2:30 p.m., in room 2172, Rayburn House Office Building, Hon. Ted Yoho (chairman of the subcommittee) presiding.

Mr. YOHO. Good afternoon. The subcommittee will come to order.

Members present will be permitted to submit written statements to be included in the official hearing record. Without objection, the hearing record will remain open for 5 calendar days to allow statements, questions, and extraneous material for the record subject to length limitations in the rules.

As a reminder, I would like to remind the audience members that disruption of the committee proceedings is against the law and will not be tolerated. Although wearing theme shirts while seated in the hearing room is permissible, holding up signs during the meeting proceedings is not. Any disruptions will result in the suspension of the proceedings until the capitol police can restore order. And we thank you for following these guidelines.

Good afternoon, and thank you to everyone for joining us today to discuss this sobering topic. The latest outbreak of ethnic violence in Burma's Rakhine state has brought about the most urgent humanitarian emergency in the Asia Pacific today.

We are convening this hearing today for two primary purposes. First, to gather information and impressions from our expert panel, some of whom recently have been on the ground in Burma to see this firsthand. And, secondly, to hear their recommendations for how the U.S. policy can best address this crisis.

The Rohingya, a stateless Muslim people living in the Rakhine state, are frequently described as the world's most persecuted minority. Denied citizenship in Burma and treated as unwanted, illegal immigrants, their modern history has been a continuous deprivation of basic human rights, punctuated with episodes of extreme violence. The latest of these is ongoing, and it is just unbelievable the amount of persecution that is going on.

On August 25, the Arakan Rohingya Salvation Army, ARSA, a Rohingya militant group, launched a coordinated attack on a security outpost in Burma's Rakhine state, killing approximately a dozen personnel. In the weeks that have followed, the Burmese military has carried out a brutal retaliatory crackdown against the Rohingya population as a whole, characterized by sickening crimes against humanity.

Human Rights Watch released a report on Monday documenting widespread and systematic attacks on the Rohingya civilians; deportations and forced population transfers; murders, including the murder of women and children; sexual violence; the razing of villages; and the deployment of landmines along paths used by the refugees. The reporting is corroborated by eyewitness accounts on the ground and satellite images, and it is heart-wrenching in its details.

The military's violence has sparked a massive refugee outflow into neighboring Bangladesh, which the Economist reports is the most intense since the Rwanda genocide. In this latest crisis alone, about 436,000 Rohingya have crossed the border, overwhelming the aid organizations there and bringing the total number of Rohingya refugees in Bangladesh to near 1 million. An unknown number of additional Rohingya remain internally displaced within the Rakhine state. The death toll is in the hundreds at least, and that is at a minimum. But aid organizations and reporters are denied access to this affected area, and the total number may be much higher in the tens of thousands.

The road ahead will be difficult. Responding to the immediate crisis will be an enormous task, to say nothing of a sustainable lasting solution to the Rohingya dilemma. Burma has not created a space for the Rohingya in its society, and there is little appetite among the Buddhist majority to do so. State Counselor Aung San Suu Kyi, once thought as a global symbol of human rights and democracy, has led a lackluster response by the Burmese Government, focusing on denial and blaming the victims.

The ARSA militants are also not helping their fellow Rohingya. Their latest attack came on the very day a commission headed by the former U.N. Secretary General Kofi Annan released his recommendations on easing ethnic tensions in Rakhine. This was the government's most high-profile effort to improve the conditions in Rakhine following previous episodes of violence, and the ARSA attacked just as Aung San Suu Kyi pledged to implement the panel's recommendations.

Recent reports have indicated that the outflow of refugees to Bangladesh has slowed or stopped, which foreshadows the next stage of the crisis: The enormous challenge for humanitarian aid organizations to shift from lifesaving measures to a longer term effort to house and feed almost 1 million people, who under the current circumstances, are totally incapable of seeing to their own needs.

In Washington, we will need to determine how we can best support these efforts, as well as what policy options are available for pressuring the Burmese military to stop its brutal violence and encouraging the civilian government to take a firmer stand against the military's atrocities.

So I thank the witnesses for joining us today and look forward to their testimony and recommendations.

Without objection, the written statements will be entered into the hearing.

I now turn to the ranking member for any remarks he may have.
[The prepared statement of Mr. Yoho follows:]

Burma's Brutal Campaign Against the Rohingya
Subcommittee on Asia and the Pacific
House Committee on Foreign Affairs
Thursday, September 27, 2017, 2:30 p.m.
Opening Statement of Chairman Ted Yoho

Good afternoon, and thank you to everyone for joining us today to discuss this sobering topic. The latest outbreak of ethnic violence in Burma's Rakhine state has brought about the most urgent humanitarian emergency in the Asia-Pacific today. We are convening this hearing for two primary purposes: to gather information and impressions from our expert panel, some of whom have recently been on the ground in Burma, and hear their recommendations for how U.S. policy can best address this crisis.

The Rohingya, a stateless Muslim people living in Rakhine state, are frequently described as the world's most persecuted minority. Denied citizenship in Burma and treated as unwanted illegal immigrants, their modern history has been a continuous deprivation of basic human rights, punctuated with episodes of extreme violence. The latest of these is ongoing.

On August 25, the Arakan Rohingya Salvation Army, a Rohingya militant group, launched a coordinated attack on security outposts in Burma's Rakhine state, killing around a dozen personnel. In the weeks that have followed, the Burmese military has carried out a brutal, retaliatory crackdown against the Rohingya population as a whole, characterized by sickening crimes against humanity.

Human Rights Watch released a report on Monday documenting widespread and systematic attacks on Rohingya civilians, deportations and forced population transfers, murders including the murder of women and children, sexual violence, the razing of villages, and the deployment of landmines along paths used by refugees. Their reporting is corroborated by eyewitness accounts and satellite images, and is heart wrenching in its detail.

The military's violence has sparked a massive refugee outflow into neighboring Bangladesh, which the *Economist* reports is the most intense since the Rwandan genocide. In this latest crisis alone, about 436,000 Rohingya have crossed the border, overwhelming the aid organizations there and bringing the total number of Rohingya refugees in Bangladesh to near one million. An unknown number of additional Rohingya remain internally displaced within Rakhine state. The death toll is in the hundreds at least, but aid organizations and reporters are denied access to the affected areas, and the total may be much higher.

The road ahead will be difficult. Responding to the immediate crisis will be an enormous task, to say nothing of a sustainable, lasting solution to the Rohingya's dilemma. Burma has not created a space for the Rohingya in its society, and there is little appetite amongst the Buddhist majority to do so. State Counselor Aung San Suu Kyi, once thought of as a global symbol of human rights and democracy, has led a lackluster response by the Burmese government, focusing on denial and blaming the victims.

The ARSA militants are also not helping their fellow Rohingya. Their latest attack came on the very day a commission headed by former UN Secretary General Kofi Annan released its recommendations on easing ethnic tensions in Rakhine. This was the government's most high-profile effort to improve the conditions in Rakhine following previous episodes of violence, and ARSA attacked just as Aung San Suu Kyi pledged to implement the panel's recommendations.

Recent reports have indicated that the outflow of refugees to Bangladesh has slowed or stopped, which foreshadows the next stage of the crisis: the enormous challenge for humanitarian aid organizations to shift from lifesaving measures to a longer term effort to house and feed almost a million people who, under the current circumstances, are totally incapable of seeing to their own needs.

In Washington, we will need to determine how we can best support these efforts, as well as what policy options are available for pressuring the Burmese military to stop its brutal violence and encouraging the civilian government to take a firmer stand against the military's atrocities. So, I thank the witnesses for joining us today and look forward to their testimony and recommendations.

Mr. SHERMAN. Thank you, Mr. Chairman.

I am told that the Ambassador from Bangladesh is here. Thank you, sir, for being here, but more importantly, thank you for what your country, one of the poorest countries in the world, is doing to take care of hundreds of thousands of refugees.

I would also like to introduce the Ambassador of Burma, but, unfortunately, I can't because that Ambassador is not here. If that Ambassador were here, that Ambassador could find out what the world thinks of the policy of the Burmese Government toward hundreds of thousands of its own citizens.

A humanitarian tragedy is unfolding in Burma, which is also referred to as Myanmar. Burma's military, the Tatmadaw, moved against the Rohingya population after an August 25 attack by Rohingya militants on Burmese security forces. Nearly ½ million Rohingya Muslim refugees have fled their homeland in the Rakhine state following Burmese military operations against them.

The U.N. High Commission for Human Rights noted that this situation seems to be a textbook example of ethnic cleansing. Late last year, something similar occurred on a smaller scale when an estimated 60,000 to 90,000 Rohingyas fled to Bangladesh as a result of Burmese military operations that have followed in October 2016 Rohingya militant attack on border police.

The vast majority of those who fled to Bangladesh, which is, as I pointed out, already impoverished and overcrowded, though the vast majority have fled there, a roughly 40,000 fled to India. Unfortunately, media reports indicate that India's border security forces are attempting to prevent Rohingya from entering India through Bangladesh amidst the ongoing exodus from Burma, including the reported use of stun guns and pepper grenades. However, I should point out that the international law is different for Bangladesh, which is the first resting place of those fleeing. Once people are in Bangladesh, they are not being oppressed, although they are not economically viable at the present time. So whether India has an obligation to accept them from Bangladesh is a subject that perhaps our witnesses can get into.

The United States has led an international response to protect the—we have lead the international response to protect Muslims in Kosovo and in Bosnia against Serb aggression. We need to play a role along with others in protecting the Rohingya in dealing with the humanitarian needs. We also need to make sure that the Muslim world realizes that we are the only country to bomb a Christian nation, Serbia, for the defense of Muslims, something that is not widely focused on in the Muslim world.

The administration should work to ensure that the physical needs of hundreds of thousands of refugees are provided for, secure a halt to Burmese military operations against the Rohingya, secure a safe return of the Rohingya population back to Burma, demand that Burma end decades of discrimination against the Rohingya, including addressing cases of appropriated land, citizenship rights, political representation, the lack of free movement, and economic improvements. This is especially necessary in citizenship rights. The idea that a people could live in a country generation after generation and still be called foreigners under that country's laws is simply outrageous.

We are to urge the United Nations Security Council to establish a U.N. Security Council probe commission on Burmese ethnic cleansing against the Rohingya and urge the United Nations Security Council to establish a U.N.-monitored safe zone for the Rohingya in Rakhine state to protect it from future mass killings.

The Burmese Government says it will allow the return of these refugees, catch-22, when they provide proof of nationality. Since 1982, the Burmese Government has stripped the Rohingya of their citizenship, making it impossible for them to prove their Burmese nationality. This is outrageous. Every group of people on the Earth has immigrated to where they live from somewhere else. Since we all came from apparently eastern Africa, and to say that you are not a citizen of a country because you cannot prove that your most ancient ancestors were born there would make us all citizens perhaps of Ethiopia and not citizens of any other country in the world. I say that just to show how absurd the position is to deny citizenship for people not only born in the country, but whose parents, even grandparents were born in that country.

The United States, who was closely involved in bringing democracy to Burma, in a process that included elections in 2010 and 2015, the release of political prisoners, the formation of a civilian government, and the lifting of U.N. sanctions. The United States should also take the lead of holding democratic practices, and democracy goes with fair treatment of minorities and a protection of minorities. It must press the Burmese Government to end military operations against the Rohingya, accept the refugees back, and grant them citizenship. I think they are already legally citizens. Recognize that citizenship.

In September of last year, I, along with other members of this subcommittee, met with Aung San Suu Kyi as the former administration decided to lift a number of economic sanctions on Burma. It is clear, after the massacres and cleansing of October 2016 and the recent actions, that we need to reevaluate that policy.

Last week, the State Department announced the U.S. is providing an additional 32 million in humanitarian assistance. I look forward to hearing from our witnesses whether that is sufficient.

And I yield back.

Mr. YOHO. I thank the ranking member.

I too also would like to welcome Ambassador Ziauddin. Thank you for being here, for representing Bangladesh, and thank you for the support you have given to this crisis that is ongoing.

I would like to commend the ranking member on his pointing out that the United States is a Nation that is—the only nation that has bombed a Christian nation to protect the Muslim populace.

With that, I would like to turn to Mr. Chabot from Ohio for an opening statement.

Mr. CHABOT. Thank you very much, Mr. Chairman, and thank you for holding this really very important hearing at a critical time.

The news, as you indicated, from the Rakhine state about the humanitarian crisis, unfortunately, seems to be getting worse every day. As a former chairman of this committee, I have been following this with really great concern for some time now.

The previous administration touted Burma as a success story and relaxed many of the restrictions that have been longstanding, including on the Burmese military. Unfortunately, we are seeing that, in many ways, the Burma that we see today isn't that much different than the one that we knew only a few years ago. There have been some improvements, but far too few.

A number of us at the time were warned that this democratic transformation was incomplete and that President Obama and then Secretary of State Clinton's optimism was premature. The current situation in Rakhine state, unfortunately, seems to illustrate that we were right, much as I wish that we had been wrong.

So I look very much forward to this very distinguished panel here and hearing what solutions, what we can do to help. So I thank you. I yield back.

Mr. YOHO. Thank you, Mr. Chabot.

Now we will go to Mr. Rohrabacher for an opening statement.

Mr. ROHRABACHER. I have been following the events in this part of the world for a number of decades, but I will have to admit that I have a very shallow information base, knowledge base on what is happening on the issue being described today. So I will be very interested in hearing a history of this.

I realize that I have been very active in the past in trying to support the Karens and the Karenis who were brutalized by the Burmese Government. And the Karens and the Kareni, of course, are Christians, or at least a large segment of their population is Christian. I understand from the people I know in Burma that there is a great deal of brutality still going on by the Burmese Government toward the Karens and the Kareni. However, being Christians,

7

they don't seem to get as much attention as it is when we see a group of Muslims who are under attack.

I think that it is up to us to send a message to Burma that this type of repression, both whether it is Christians or Muslim, that attacks on unarmed civilians is unacceptable. But let me also note that we need to send a message to the people, to the Muslim people of the world that our human rights agenda is not just a front to attack Muslim regimes when they are doing something wrong, but when the Islamic people are being victimized, that we care about them just as we do anyone else.

So I thank you for this hearing today. I plan to educate myself from what we are going to hear from the witnesses. So thank you very much.

Mr. YOHO. Thank you, Mr. Rohrabacher.

Now we will go to Mrs. Ann Wagner for an opening statement.

Mrs. WAGNER. Thank you, Mr. Chairman, for hosting this hearing. I too am devastated by the news coming out of Burma.

For over 60 years, the Burmese Government has persecuted religious and ethnic minorities across the country. War has raged in Karen states, Chin states, Shan states, Kachin states, and the list goes on and on.

The Obama administration lifted sanctions. Actually, Burma was becoming a democracy, but Burma's Government had no authority over the nation's powerful military. Human rights and democracy activists across Burma feel abandoned. The Christians in Kachin states have been ignored by the West. The Rohingya Muslims have been left for dead. With more Rohingya now living outside of Burma than living inside of Burma, the international community must stop demanding action and take action. We are in part to blame for not holding the Burmese Government and military accountable for their actions.

So I want to thank you all very much for coming today. And a special thanks to Mr. Sullivan and to Ms. Gittleman for the advocacy work that you do in this arena. And my sincere thanks to the Ambassador from Bangladesh for the generosity of your country in opening up your border.

Mr. Chairman, I yield back.

Mr. YOHO. Thank you, Mrs. Wagner.

This hearing today is so important because of the atrocities that going on out there, and we depend on the information that you guys give us, the panel, on the direction we go. When we look at the history of this, the length of time this has been going on, I don't know how the world can stand by and do nothing. And so you guys are going to bring this out into the open. And I don't want to say you are not doing anything because you are the Ambassadors, you are dealing with this in a good way, and we commend you. But we have to bring a stop to this. This is the 21st century, and we are doing stuff from the stone age to people on the ground.

We met with an NGO yesterday, and he was showing us graphic pictures of charred bodies that were lined up, people with flamethrowers burning people in the 21st century. It is unacceptable, and we need to bring this to an end with the world community.

So with that, I look forward to your testimonies. And I want you to understand that so much of what you guys tell us in a hearing goes into legislation that we put on through the State Department, maybe the Treasury or other organizations, so be very specific, be bold. I give you the permission. You can direct us. Use this opportunity to say, if I could write the legislation, this is what I would do to bring this to an end. So I welcome your testimonies.

You are limited to about 5 minutes. Try to end when the red light goes on or ends at 5 minutes. Make sure you press your button so the microphone is on.

With that, I am going to introduce the panel. We are going to start with Dr. Michael Martin, specialist in Asian affairs for the Congressional Research Service, Foreign Affairs, Defense, and Trade Division. Thank you for being here. Mr. Walter Lohman, thank you for being back. Director of the Asian Studies Center for the Heritage Foundation. Dr. Daniel Sullivan, senior advocate for human rights at the Refugee International. And Ms. Andrea Gittleman, program manager for the Simon-Skjodt Center for the Prevention of Genocide at the U.S. Holocaust Memorial Museum. That is a mouthful. Thank you for being here.

And, Dr. Martin, if you don't mind, we will start with you, and look forward to hearing from you.

STATEMENT OF MICHAEL F. MARTIN, PH.D., SPECIALIST IN ASIAN AFFAIRS, FOREIGN AFFAIRS, DEFENSE, AND TRADE DIVISION, CONGRESSIONAL RESEARCH SERVICE

Mr. MARTIN. Chairman Yoho, Ranking Member Sherman, and the members of the subcommittee, thank you for this opportunity to appear before you today to discuss the current crisis in Burma's Rakhine state, the status of the Rohingya who have fled to Bangladesh, as well as those remaining in Burma.

The current crisis in Burma's Rakhine state is not the first time in which thousands of Rohingya have fled to Bangladesh, nor is it the only crisis in Burma that involves forced displacement for thousands of Burmans from their home.

According to the United Nations High Commissioner for Refugees, there were over 375,000 internally displaced persons in Burma at the end of 2016 due to the nation's ongoing civil war. In addition, more than 100,000 refugees live in camps in Thailand as a result of past fighting in Karen, Kareni, Mon, and Shan states. Some of these refugees have been living in camps for over 30 years.

While Burma's civil war and ongoing humanitarian challenges are issues in their own rights, it is the plight of the Rohingya that has captured the world's attention.

Since Burma's military junta, the State Peace and Development Council transferred power to a mixed civilian military government in 2011, large-scale forced displacement of Rohingya have occurred on four occasions from June to October 2012, again in the spring of 2015, during the winter of 2016-2017, and most recently, starting on August 25, 2017. The latest displacement began after the Arakan Rohingya Salvation Army, or ARSA, allegedly attacked 30 security outposts northern Rakhine state. Burma's military, or Tatmadaw, responded by initiating a clearance operation in the townships of Buthidaung, Maungdaw, and Rathedaung. As a result, over half of Burma's estimated 1.1 million Rohingya are now

in refugee camps in Bangladesh, and I would add that that percentage is probably low.

During my 2-week trip to Burma earlier this month, I visited
three camps of internally displaced persons, or IDPs, in northern
Shan state. I also interviewed six individuals who said they had
been beaten by Tatmadaw soldiers for their alleged support of ethnic armed organizations, or EAOs, operating near their villages.
Their stories of abuse at the hands of the Tatmadaw were amaz-
ingly similar, maybe not surprisingly similar, to those being told by
the Rohingya right now in Bangladesh. I would also add that none
of them accounted similar beatings by EAO soldiers.

During my trip, I was repeatedly told that most Burmans, including other ethnic minorities, welcome the Tatmadaw's clearance
operation and the resulting displacement of the Rohingya. The popular narrative among Burmans is that the Rohingya are Bengalis,
illegal immigrants from Bangladesh, and are part of an effort to
transform Burma into a Muslim nation, as was done in Indonesia
and Malaysia centuries ago. When asked, people discredit claims of
misconduct by the Tatmadaw soldiers and attribute any human
rights abuses to ARSA.

While many international observers have criticized State Counselor Aung San Suu Kyi for her failure to take action, few have directed their criticism at Burma's Commander in Chief, Senior General Min Aung Hlaing. Under Burma's 2008 constitution, a constitution written by the Tatmadaw, General Min Aung Hlaing has
supreme authority over all of Burma's security forces, including the
Tatmadaw, border guard forces, and the Myanmar police force.
State Counselor Aung San Suu Kyi and the civilian government
have little direct authority over those security forces.

The events of the past month in Burma raised a number of potential issues for Congress. Congress may consider the immediate
humanitarian crisis in Bangladesh and Burma, as well as the possible long-term assistance that may be required. Congress may also
address whether allegations of human rights abuses by the Burmese security forces, ARSA, or others in Rakhine states can be
properly investigated, and if found credible, adjudicated in an ap-
propriate manner.

In addition, this crisis provides an opportunity for the United
States to reflect on its policy toward Burma in general. The events
in Rakhine state reveal much about the relationship between the
Tatmadaw and Aung San Suu Kyi and her government, as well as
relations among Burma's various ethnic groups and the nation's
prospects for peace. It has also raised question about Burma's role
in regional geopolitical strategic and security relations, including
those with China and India.

Mr. Chairman, this concludes my oral remarks. Thank you again
for the opportunity to testify. I look forward to the subcommittee's
questions on either my oral or written testimony.

[The prepared statement of Mr. Martin follows:]

Statement of

Michael F. Martin
Specialist in Asian Affairs

Before

Committee on Foreign Affairs
Subcommittee on Asia and the Pacific
U.S. House of Representatives

Hearing on

"Burma's Brutal Campaign Against the Rohingya"

September 26, 2017

Congressional Research Service
7-5700
www.crs.gov
<Product Code>

Chairman Yoho, Ranking Member Sherman, and Members of the Subcommittee, thank you for the opportunity to appear before you today to discuss the current crisis in Burma's Rakhine State, and the situation of the Rohingya, both those who have fled to Bangladesh, as well as those remaining in Burma. My name is Michael F. Martin, and I am testifying today in my capacity as an analyst for the Congressional Research Service.

The events unfolding in Burma's Rakhine State – entailing an estimated 430,000 predominately Sunni Muslim Rohingya have fled into Bangladesh, tens of thousands of Rohingya, Rakhine and other ethnic minorities who have been displaced from their villages into temporary camps within Rakhine State, and possibly more than a thousand people who have been killed – is not the first such crisis for the region. Mass displacements of Rohingya from Rakhine State have occurred periodically dating back at least to 1978. Nor is Rakhine the only state in Burma in which conflict is forcing farmers out of their villages and into temporary camps. Burma's 70-year old civil war continues in Kachin and Shan State, where Burma's military, or Tatmadaw, and various ethnic armed organizations, or EAOs, fight for control of land and valuable mineral resources.

The current displacement of Rohingya began after a new EAO, the Arakan Rohiungya Salvation Army (ARSA) reportedly attacked 30 security outposts along the border with Bangladesh on August 25, 2017, killing over a dozen Burmese police officers and at least one Tatmadaw soldier. In response, ARSA was officially declared a terrorist organization, the first time Burma used such a declaration for an insurgent group. In addition, the Tatmadaw deployed more than 70 battalions, or an estimated 30,000-35,000 soldiers, into Rakhine State. The ensuing "clearance operation" in the townships of Buthidaung, Maungdaw, and Rathedaung in northern Rakhine State has contributed to the large-scale displacement of Rohingya, as well as the displacement of other ethnic groups, such as the Rakhine, Hindi, Dyna, Magyi, Mro, and Thet.

Some of the Rohingya who have made it to informal refugee camps in Bangladesh claim that Tatmadaw soldiers entered their villages, and proceeded to shoot civilians, rape women, and then burn down the entire village. International medical teams treating the Rohingya in these camps report that some people bear gunshot wounds consistent with being shot from behind, while some women have injuries consistent with sexual assault. The Tatmadaw has denied that its soldiers are killing civilians, raping women, and burning villages. According to the Tatmadaw, the only casualties are "ARSA terrorists" and the villages are being destroyed by ARSA and its sympathizers. In her televised speech of September 19, 2017, State Counsellor Aung San Suu Kyi stated:

> We condemn all human rights violations and the unlawful violence. We are committed to the restoration of peace, stability, and the rule of law throughout the state. The security forces have been instructed to adhere strictly to the code of conduct in carrying out security operations, to exercise all due restraint, and to take full measures to avoid collateral damage and the harming of innocent civilians. Human rights violations and all other acts that affect the stability and harmony and undermine the rule of law will be addressed in accordance with the strict norms of justice.

It is difficult to know for certain what has taken place in the townships of northern Rakhine State as media and humanitarian assistance access to the region has been largely cut off by the Tatmadaw for security reasons. Satellite imagery of the region shows evidence that dozens of villages in Maungdaw Township have been partially or totally burned down, and a smaller number of villages in Buthidaung and Rathedaung townships display varying degrees of fire damage. One BBC reporter who obtained access to the area witnessed the looting and destruction of a Rohingya village by what appeared to be a group of Rakhine men. The Tatmadaw soldiers escorting the reporter took no measures to interrogate or detain the Rakhine men.

Although the pace has slowed, the number of Rohingya entering Bangladesh increases every day. Over the past year, approximately half of the estimated 1.1 million Rohingya residing in Burma have fled to Bangladesh. To understand why Rohingya exoduses of this sort repeatedly happens in Rakhine State, one has to know about the history of the Rohingya and of past large scale displacements, the competing narratives in Burma about the Rohingya, the Burmese government's policies regarding the Rohingya, and the attitudes and culture of the Tatmadaw with regard to the Rohingya, and ethnic minorities in general.

Recent Mass Displacements of Rohingya

The history of recent large-scale exoduses of Rohingya from Rakhine State dates back at least to February 1978, when Burma's ruling military junta, under the leadership of General Ne Win, launched Operation Naga Min, or Operation King Dragon, ostensibly designed to expel a group of Rohingya insurgents, the Rohingya Patriotic Front (RPF), from northern Rakhine State. Over a period of three months, Tatmadaw soldiers swept through northern Rakhine State, and an estimated 200,000 – 250,000 Rohingya fled to Bangladesh, where they found shelter in temporary camps near Cox's Bazar. The United Nations High Commissioner for Refugees (UNHCR) recognized the Rohingya as refugees, and was able to secure Bangladesh's support for the establishment of two official refugee camps. Most of the Rohingya were able to return to Burma following negotiations between Bangladesh, Burma and the United Nations.

The Tatmadaw conducted another counter-insurgent campaign in northern Rakhine State in the winter of 1992 against the Rohingya Solidarity Organization, an offshoot of the RPF. By April 1992, more than 250,000 Rohingya had fled to Bangladesh to escape the military operations. As happened in 1978, many of the Rohingya returned to Burma after the military campaign was over, but some remained in the refugee camps in Bangladesh.

From June to October 2012, approximately 200,000 Rohingya fled to Bangladesh, and another 120,000 ended up in internally displaced persons (IDP) camps in Rakhine State after rioting erupted between the Rohingya and largely Buddhist Rakhine population in Rakhine State. The Tatmadaw responded by bringing in troops to restore law and order. While many of the Rohingya in Bangladesh were eventually able to return to Burma, those in IDP camps have been unable to return to their villages.

In the spring of 2015, an estimated 25,000 people – many of whom were Rohingya from Rakhine State – took to boats in the Andaman Sea in hopes of reaching Malaysia and Thailand. Hundreds died along the way. A small number of the surviving emigres returned to Burma, but most have chosen to remain in exile.

In late 2016, following the alleged attacks on three border outposts by the Arakan Rohingya Salvation Army (ARSA), approximately 87,000 Rohingya crossed into Bangladesh to escape the ensuing "clearance operation" conducted by the Tatmadaw. The media, human rights organizations, and international humanitarian organizations accused the Tatmadaw of serious human rights abuses during the "clearance operation." The Tatmadaw denied these allegations.

State Counsellor Aung San Suu Kyi responded to the 2016 events by forming an international commission, the Advisory Commission on Rakhine State, headed by former UN General Secretary Kofi Annan, to "identify the factors that have resulted in violence, displacement, and underdevelopment" in Rakhine State. On August 24, 2017, the Commission released its final report, cautioning that "a highly militarized response is unlikely to bring peace to the area." Among the Commission's recommendations are to promote greater economic development in Rakhine State, to align Burma's 1982 Citizenship Law with international standards and enable the Rohingya to obtain citizenship, and make arrangements for the resettlement of IDPs. In March 2017, the UN Human Rights Council approved a fact-finding mission to investigate alleged human rights violations in Rakhine State, but Aung San Suu Kyi has so far refused to permit the mission entry into Burma, stating that their presence "would have created greater hostility between the different communities."

With the exception of the 2015 exodus, the mass displacements of Rohingyas has corresponded with large-scale deployments of Tatmadaw soldiers into northern Rakhine State. In each case, the media, human rights organizations, and international humanitarian assistance organizations have reported evidence of serious human rights abuses of the Rohingya by the Tatmadaw soldiers. The Tatmadaw has repeatedly denied these allegations.

Competing Narratives

Historical evidence shows that a Muslim community has lived in northern Rakhine State for centuries, although not initially identified as Rohingya. Muslim merchants and traders settled in what is now eastern Bangladesh and Burma's Rakhine State as early as the 8th Century. The Kingdom of Mrauk-U ruled this region from 1429 to 1785, as a joint Buddhist-Muslim society, under the protection of the Islamic Bengal Sultanate, and with a significant Muslim population. In 1785, the Bamar Konbaung Dynasty conquered the Kingdom of Mrauk-U, and ruled the area until the British extended the British Raj into Burma in 1824. During the time of British rule over Burma, an unknown number of Muslims migrated into northern Rakhine State in what the British considered an internal resettlement, but which the Tatmadaw and much of the Burmese population now consider illegal immigration.

It is uncertain when a portion of the Muslim community of Rakhine State began identifying itself as Rohingya (There is a separate Muslim community in Rakhine State known as the Kamar, which is considered an indigenous ethnic group by the Burmese government.) According to the Rohingya narrative, the notion of a Rohingya ethnic group dates at least as far back as Burma's independence in 1948. During the period of civilian rule in Burma (1948-1962), Rohingya were Members of Parliament, served in the Tatmadaw, and worked as civil servants. This ended after the Tatmadaw took control of the government in 1962, and began its anti-Rohingya campaigns.

Most people in Burma – including the majority ethnic Bamar and the various ethnic minorities – tell a different narrative about the origins of what they refer to as the "Bengalis" of Rakhine State. Most people in Burma do not consider the Rohingya a legitimate ethnic community that has lived in Rakhine State for centuries. Instead, they assert that the Bengalis are illegal immigrants from Bangladesh or India that entered Rakhine State during the time of British rule or more recently across the porous border with Bangladesh. In addition, Burma's Buddhist nationalist movement, Ma Ba Tha, and its outspoken leader, Ashin Wirathu, portray the "Bengalis" as the point of a spear of an effort by global Islam to transform Burma from a predominately Buddhist nation into an Islamic state. As a result, the Rohingya are widely seen as a threat to Burma's identity as a Buddhist nation of Southeast Asia.

This popular narrative has translated into popular support for the Tatmadaw's clearance operation in northern Rakhine State and approval of the resulting large-scale displacement of the Rohingya. Many people in Burma believe the Tatmadaw's assertions that its troops have not engaged in human rights abuses during the various clearance operations, and think the international media is intentionally spreading false stories about such matters. Commander-in-Chief Senior General Min Aung Hlaing is reportedly popular in most of Burma, even in some ethnic minority areas, because of his strong response to the "ARSA terrorist threat" and the resulting return of the so-called "Bengalis" to Bangladesh.

Burmese Government Policies on the Rohingya

The Burmese government – whether under military-rule or under the current mixed civilian-military government – has established a number of discriminatory policies specifically toward the Rohingya. Among these policies are:

- **Denial of Citizenship** – In 1982, Burma's military junta replaced the 1948 Union Citizenship Act with a new law, the 1982 Citizenship Law, that effectively revoked the citizenship of most of the Rohingya in Burma, rendering them stateless.

- **Denial of Suffrage and Representation** – In 2015, then-President Thein Sein invalidated the temporary identification cards ("white cards") possessed by many Rohingya that had permitted them to vote in past elections. As a result, Union Election Commission did not allow the Rohingya to vote in the 2015 parliamentary elections, and prohibited Rohingya political parties and candidates from running for office in the elections.

- **Denial of Education and Employment** – Because they are not citizens, most Rohingyas cannot attend public universities, work for the government, or join the military or the Myanmar Police Force.

- **Restrictions on Movement** – Rohingya in rural areas are prohibited from moving out of their home villages without the permission of local authorities.

- **Restrictions on Marriage, Religious Conversion and Procreation** – In 2015, Burma's Union Parliament passed the four "Race and Religion Protection Laws" that seemingly targeted Burma's Muslim population and, in particular, the Rohingya. The laws banned cohabitation with someone who is not one's spouse (to ban de facto polygamy), prohibited interfaith marriages and conversion to Islam within a marriage without government approval, and required that women living in certain regions – regions with a high percentage of Muslim households – space pregnancies at least 36 months apart.

Tatmadaw Attitudes toward the Rohingya

After the Tatmadaw seized power from an elected civilian government in 1962, Burma's military junta engaged in a series of activities that demonstrated an apparent antipathy toward the Rohingya. In particular, junta leader General Ne Win seemingly harbored a strong animosity toward the Rohingya. Under General Ne Win's command, Burmese forces conducted several military operations in northern Rakhine State targeted at the Rohingya community, including Operation King Dragon in 1978. General Ne Win reportedly supported the 1982 Citizenship Act that stripped most Rohingya of their citizenship, and implemented government policies designed to restrict their civil liberties. The Tatmadaw has been one of the most consistent advocates of the idea that the Rohingya are illegal immigrants from Bangladesh, and are not an indigenous ethnic minority in Burma.

The various military operations in northern Rakhine State have consistently resulted in the forced displacement of thousands of Rohingyas, and usually have involved credible allegations of serious human rights violations of Rohingya by Tatmadaw soldiers. Some Tatmadaw officers have defended their soldiers accused of raping Rohingya women by stating that Rohingya women are too dirty and ugly for their soldiers to even consider raping. In general, the Tatmadaw speak of and seemingly consider the Rohingya as inferior to the Bamar majority, and by extension, seem to tolerate discrimination and maltreatment of Rohingya.

One lingering question is the goal or objective of the Tatmadaw's treatment of the Rohingya. Some observers, including U.N. High Commissioner for Human Rights Zeid Ra'ad Al Hussein, think the Tatmadaw's activities constitute "ethnic cleansing" of Rohingya from Burma, and the ultimate goal is the removal of all Rohingya. Others maintain the objective is to reduce the percentage of Rohingya in northern Rakhine State by forced displacement plus the immigration of Bamar, Rakhine and other ethnic minorities into the region.

One possible indication of the Tatmadaw's goal may be how the Burmese government manages the return of the displace Rohingya. Aung San Suu Kyi has indicated that the return will be managed in accordance with a 1992 agreement between Bangladesh and Burma on a previous case of mass displacement. That agreement stipulated that Burma would accept the return of anyone who could provide evidence of their prior residence in Burma. One Burmese official has stated that this may mean proof of eligibility for Burmese citizenship, which would significantly reduce the number of Rohingya who would be permitted to return to Burma.

Issues for U.S. Policy

The current crisis in Rakhine State raises a number of questions regarding U.S. policy toward Burma and Bangladesh. The following list of questions is not meant to be exhaustive, but more indicative of the breadth and scope of factors that Congress may wish to bear in mind when examining U.S. policy toward Burma and Bangladesh.

- The State Department has announced an additional $32 million in humanitarian assistance in response to the situation in Rakhine State, with most of the funds going to help refugees in Bangladesh. What efforts are being made to obtain similar commitments from other nations? How long will this assistance last? How much additional assistance will be needed? Is the amount being provided for assistance within Rakhine State sufficient to address current needs?

- The Burmese government has said it will lead the humanitarian response In Rakhine State and will continue to avail the support of the Red Cross Movements. What international efforts are being made to obtain greater access to the IDPs in Rakhine State? Is the Tatmadaw intentionally hindering the provision of assistance in Rakhine State? If so, what can be done to obtain access to the internally displaced people, regardless of ethnicity?

- Stories of serious human rights abuses continue to be reported from the Rohingya refugees in Bangladesh, while the Tatmadaw claim to have found a mass grave of Hindis allegedly killed by ARSA. How legitimate are these claims?

- So far, the Tatmadaw has denied its troops have engaged in human rights abuses during the clearance operations, and that any casualties are ARSA terrorists. As a result, the Tatmadaw refuse to permit any independent international investigation of the alleged human rights abuse. What effect have these allegations and the Tatmadaw's refusal to permit independent investigation had on U.S. relations with the Tatmadaw and Aung San Suu Kyi's government?

- What is the Tatmadaw's objective in Rakhine State – the total displacement of the Rohingya, a major reduction in the Rohingya population, or the reestablishment of law and order? How might the answer to this question influence U.S. policy in Burma and relations with the Tatmadaw?

- In response to the situation in Rakhine State, the United Kingdom has cut off its assistance programs with the Tatmadaw. China, India, Israel, and Russia provide the Tatmadaw with arms and military training. Commander-in-Chief Min Aung Hlaing recently traveled to Europe seeking closer military-to-military relations with several nations. What steps, if any, should the United States take with regard to Defense and State Department relations with the Tatmadaw?

- Aung San Suu Kyi has repeatedly stated that international coverage of the situation in Rakhine State is biased, inaccurate, and incomplete. Is there any merit to her claims? If so, in what respect? What impact might this have on U.S. relations with her government?

- Aung San Suu Kyi recommitted her government to the implementation of the Annan Commission recommendations in her speech last week. What, if anything, can the United States do to assist in the implementation of those recommendations?

- Little is known for certain about ARSA. What do we know about its origins, funding, size, and alleged relations with international Islamic fundamentalist organizations? What are the implications for U.S. counter-terrorism efforts in South and Southeast Asia?

- What impact has the recent outbreak of violence had on the ongoing conflict in Kachin and Shan State, as well as efforts to advance the political dialogue to resolve that conflict? Is there any evidence that the various EAOs are concerned that the Tatmadaw is emboldened by the popularity of its activities in Rakhine State and may extend such an approach to eastern Burma? What are the possible implications for U.S. efforts to promote a peaceful resolution of Burma's civil war?

- China sees both economic and strategic value in its relationship with Burma. China recently completed an oil and gas pipeline that runs from China's Yunnan Province, across the conflict area in northern Shan State, and ending in the deep-water port of Kyaukphyu, near the city of Sittwe in Rakhine State. China hopes to build a rail line and highway along the same corridor, providing China with direct freight access to the Indian Ocean. What effect could and should China's economic and strategic interests in Burma have on U.S. policy?

- How might the events in Rakhine State influence U.S. relations with the Association of Southeast Asian Nations (ASEAN), as well as other nations in the region, including India, Indonesia, Malaysia, and Thailand?

Mr. Chairman, this concludes my testimony. Thank you again for the opportunity to testify, and I am most willing to respond to any questions you or other Members of the Committee may have pertaining to the subject of this hearing.

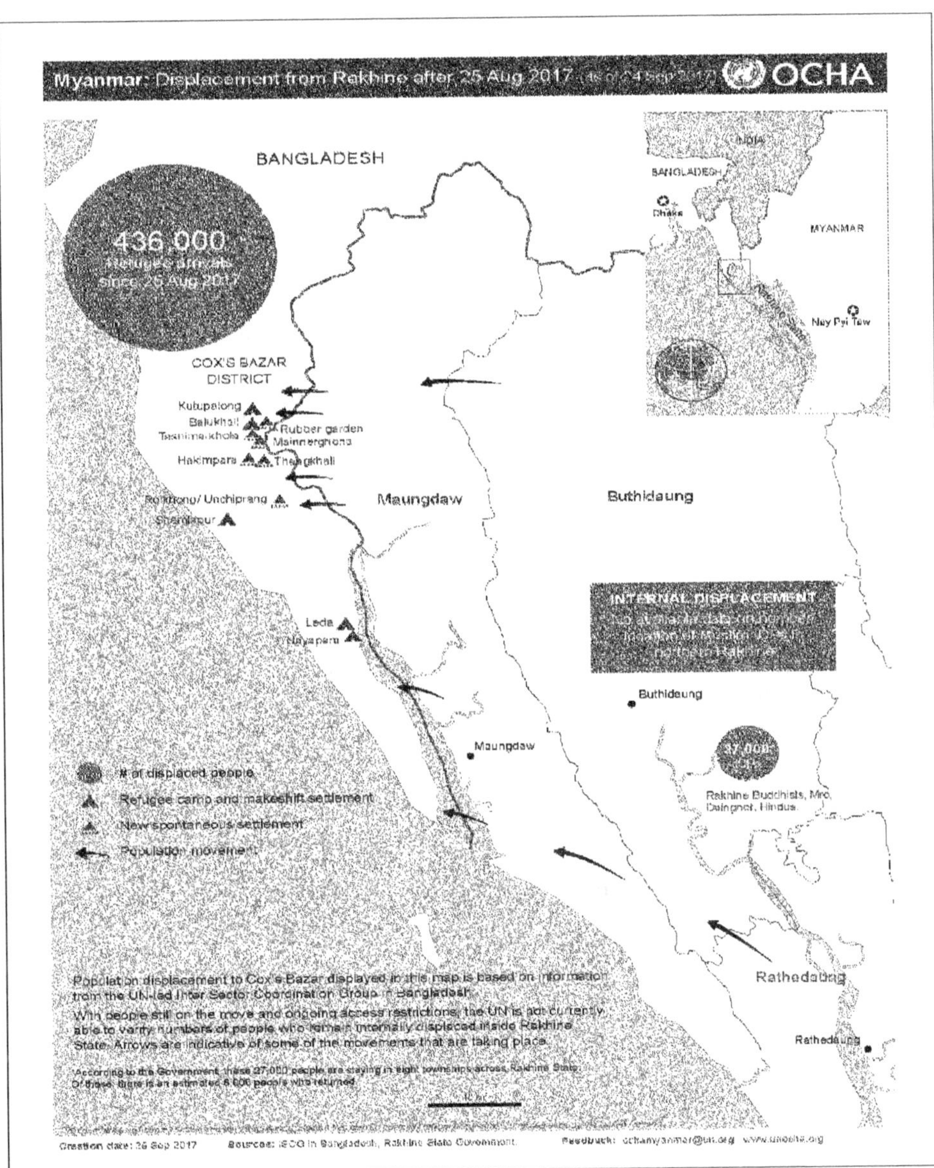
Myanmar: Displacement from Rakhine after 25 Aug 2017 (as of 24 Sep 2017)
OCHA
BANGLADESH
INDIA
BANGLADESH
Dhaka
MYANMAR
Nay Pyi Taw
436,000
Refugee arrivals
since 25 Aug 2017
COX'S BAZAR DISTRICT
Kutupalong
Balukhali
Rubber garden
Tasnimarkhola
Mainnerghona
Hakimpara
Thangkhali
Roikhong/ Unchiprang
Shamlapur
Maungdaw
Buthidaung
Leda
Nayapara
INTERNAL DISPLACEMENT
Buthidaung
Maungdaw
37,000
Rakhine Buddhists, Mro,
Daingnet, Hindus
# of displaced people
Refugee camp and makeshift settlement
New spontaneous settlement
Population movement
Rathedaung
Rathedaung
Population displacement to Cox's Bazar displayed in this map is based on information
from the UN-led Inter Sector Coordination Group in Bangladesh.
With people still on the move and ongoing access restrictions, the UN is not currently
able to verify numbers of people who remain internally displaced inside Rakhine
State. Arrows are indicative of some of the movements that are taking place.
According to the Government, these 27,000 people are staying in eight townships across Rakhine State.
Of these, there is an estimated 5,000 people who returned.
Creation date: 25 Sep 2017   Sources: ISCG in Bangladesh, Rakhine State Government   Feedback: ocha.myanmar@un.org, www.unocha.org

Mr. YOHO. Dr. Martin, I appreciate it, and thank you for that great testimony.

We have been blessed and honored to have the chairman of the full committee, Mr. Ed Royce here, and he has an opening statement.

Mr. Chairman.

Mr. ROYCE. Thank you. Thank you, Chairman Yoho, for giving me this opportunity, because I did want to register my observations about the circumstances that we are dealing with here. And I want to thank you for this important hearing, Chairman Yoho.

There are few issues more pressing that demand our attention as much as this issue does this week and last week and the week before. The plight of the Rohingya, an ethnic group that many have called the most persecuted in the world, is also one that deserved our attention a long time ago. As a matter of fact, if we went back to 1982, if we look at what this population has been through, a citizenship law denied Burmese citizenship to Rohingya, even though most of them had lived in that country for generations. They have been denied freedom of movement, denied access to an education, to healthcare. Burmese Rohingya have been marginalized by every level of government, and that is top to bottom. And today the persecution of these people have reached new horrific levels.

Fleeing government retaliation for attacks carried out by the ARSA, a fringe militant group at least 420,000 Rohingyas have been driven from their homes. They have been forced to cross the border into Bangladesh. I have heard personally their stories of what they have been through, of the villages that have been burned. Hundreds have been killed officially, but we know the number is many multiples of this. And journalists have been denied access to large areas of Rakhine state. So that is why I suspect this number is far, far higher than what is being reported.

Now, what has been reported so far is that 200 villages have been burned, but I hear reports that I haven't seen in the papers yet from others who are connected to the Internet who tell me about additional villages being burned. Landmines have been placed inside Burma's borders with Bangladesh, maiming a handful of those seeking safe haven, but we know more will be killed by these landmines because no one has made a record of where they have been placed. It is little wonder that the U.N. human rights chief called this a textbook example of ethnic cleansing, and that is a strong but very warranted condemnation.

In the face of these atrocities, Burma's response has been, frankly, appalling. I have no illusion that with a young democratically elected government the challenges facing Aung San Suu Kyi are immense. But at the same time, if she is only a counselor, and if the power and the authority actually rests with the military, she still has the responsibility to speak out strongly on this issue of human rights. She has got to bring together widely diverse ethnic groups and work to improve an economy that suffered for decades under the military junta's mismanagement. But nothing is more important than providing for the safety of the people within her borders. And Aung San Suu Kyi's recent statement questioning why the Rohingya were fleeing and denying that the military had conducted clearance operations is wildly off the mark.

The perpetrators of this ethnic cleansing must be condemned in the strongest terms and held accountable. The Burmese Government cannot be allowed to blatantly and cruelly mistreat Rohingya Muslims and other minority groups. The United States must prioritize the Rohingya and the protection of human rights in its relations with Burma, and we should use the tool at our disposal to help put a stop to this violence and to get USAID down on the ground and to get the Burmese people, the Rohingya people returned.

Lastly, Bangladesh deserves praise for opening its borders to this influx of refugees. It is my sincere hope that the government honors its promise to build shelter for new arrivals and provide the needed medical care to them.

And again, I thank Chairman Yoho. I thank the Ambassador of Bangladesh who is with us today. We appreciate what you have done, and I think this is a very important hearing. I thank the other members who are engaged in this issue for being involved. Thanks.

I yield back.

Mr. YOHO. Thank you, Chairman Royce. I appreciate your input and being here.

Mr. Lohman, if you would continue the testimony. Thank you.

STATEMENT OF MR. WALTER LOHMAN, DIRECTOR, ASIAN STUDIES CENTER, DAVIS INSTITUTE FOR NATIONAL SECURITY AND FOREIGN POLICY, THE HERITAGE FOUNDATION

Mr. LOHMAN. Thank you. Thank you, Mr. Chairman.

Mr. Sherman, other members of the committee, I appreciate you having me here to——

Mr. YOHO. Do you have your microphone on?

Mr. LOHMAN. It is on.

Mr. YOHO. Okay. Maybe move it a little closer.

Mr. LOHMAN. Okay. Events in Burma over the last month have been heartrending, but they are only a manifestation of deeper realities about Burma that must be taken into better account in U.S. policy going forward, particularly as regards any normalization of U.S. military ties.

The first reality concerns Burma's relationship with China, their relationship between their militaries in particular. To the extent the proposals to open U.S. relations with the Burmese military are about "balancing China," they vastly overestimate U.S. leverage.

The one inescapable geographical reality is that China shares a border with Burma. The Chinese have major interests at stake there, much bigger than our own: Stability along their border, access to the Indian Ocean, rights alternative to the Malacca straits in the South China Sea for their trade, and access to energy resources, securities interests. The Chinese play both sides of the fence. They supply and support insurgencies along the border, and at the same time, they maintain a close relationship with the Burmese military and the civilian government.

To maintain this position, the Chinese will compete with all the carrots and sticks they have, and they have far more than we do at this point in time on this particular place on the map. Our own efforts to engage in the military by comparison only compromise our values with little upside.

The second reality I think Congress needs to take into account is the potential for the Americans to impact the reform process in Burma, and particularly impact the way the military sees reform. As is well known, civilian authorities of Burma have no control over the military. Some have, therefore, theorized that the U.S. should give the military a stake in political reform by offering it benefits, chiefly, contact with the U.S. military. This ignores equities that the military has in not fully cooperating with future reforms. The Burmese military had its own objective for initiating reforms under the previous regime, objectives that did not encompass fundamental reform of its own sources of power or its ultimate interest in crushing the opposition.

The third reality concerns the nature of the Burmese military itself. The political environment in Burma has certainly changed. I think we have to acknowledge that. But I see no reason to believe the military has changed its own character. The textbook example of "ethnic cleansing" in Rakhine state is, in fact, a culmination of a decades long history of persecution by successive military governments in Burma. As Mike Martin pointed out, it is only different in degree from what has been happening in other ethnic areas for a very long time, and as Mr. Rohrbacher pointed out as well.

Given these realities, I think it is time for Congress to step away for a moment and take a look at a broader approach to Burma, do a reset on our Burma policy, and here are five things that you could consider.

Number one, remove authorities in the 2015 National Defense Authorization Act granting DOD authority to establish training opportunities for Burmese military personnel.

Number two, codify the embargo on the exported defense articles and services to Burma.

Number three, reimpose restrictions on Americans doing business with military-linked companies.

Number four, continue the prohibition on IMET and foreign military financing.

And number five, reimpose asset freezes and visa bans on Burmese military and give these measures basis in new laws tied to new goals that are reflective of the time.

It is Congress that dictated Burma policy for 20 years before President Obama moved to end sanctions. Congress should reassert its role and enact legislation that updates America's goals to reflect all that has changed in Burma and all that hasn't.

At Heritage, we are engaged in a project to develop a proposal to do just this, and we look forward to reporting back to you the full scope of our findings. Thank you.

[The prepared statement of Mr. Lohman follows:]

CONGRESSIONAL TESTIMONY

Burma's Brutal Campaign Against the Rohingya: Reexamining US-Burma Miltary-to-Military Relations

Testimony before the Foreign Affairs Committee,

Asia and the Pacific Subcommittee

United States House of Representatives

September 27, 2017

Walter Lohman
Director, Asian Studies Center
The Heritage Foundation

214 Massachusetts Avenue, NE • Washington, DC 20002 • (202) 546-4400 • heritage.org

Events in Burma over the last month have been heartrending. The violence committed by Burmese security forces in Rakhine state and the resulting human exodus, however, is only the manifestation of several deeper realities that must be taken into better account in U.S. policy going forward. The Obama Administration paid insufficient heed to these realities in pursuing its opening to Burma. With Congress' acquiescence and cooperation, it moved too far, too fast, leaving only closer military-to-military relations to keep the normalizing bicycle moving. Supporters of engagement have, therefore, continued to press for what they see as the next logical step in America's opening to Burma. The problem is that for several reasons, outreach to the Burmese military is ill-suited to meet American objectives. It rests on several misjudgments. Among these are the Burmese military's relationship with China, its place within Burma's reform political dynamic, and its nature as a fighting force.

China–Burma Relations

To the extent that a U.S. opening to the Burmese military is about "balancing China," it vastly overestimates U.S. leverage. The one inescapable geographical reality is that, in contrast to the United States which is at its strongest at sea in the Indo–Pacific region, China shares an unstable, porous land border with Burma. As a part of its effort to cope with this and support broader interests in its relations with Burma, China supports several ethnic armed groups (EAGs) in the vicinity of the border. Among these groups are the Kachin Independence Army (KIA) which is actively involved in conflict with the Burmese army, the Kokang Army, and the United Wa State Army (UWSA). As recently as 2015, the Kokang were widely reported to be operating from Chinese territory in military operations against the Burmese army. Perhaps more importantly, they have helped make the UWSA's 20,000–30,000 troops one of the best equipped insurgencies in the world. Support for the UWSA includes making available more than small-arms and ammunition. Heavy weaponry such as armed helicopters, armored personnel vehicles, and wheeled "tank destroyers" have also been supplied to the UWSA.[1] Chinese manufacturers have even helped give the UWSA the wherewithal to produce their own weapons and supply them to other EAGs.[2]

So Burma is an intensely local issue for China. But Burma also has major strategic implications for it. With the U.S. Navy prowling the narrow confines of the Western Pacific, a relationship with Burma offers China access to the Indian Ocean and alternative trade routes. In an attempt to diversify the routes by which crude oil reaches China, away from the Malacca Straits and South China Sea, it has built a pipeline that takes Middle East and African crude directly from the coast of Rakhine state to Southwestern China. A natural gas pipeline that pumps gas drilled offshore Rakhine to Southern China serves the same purpose, as well as helps diversify its sources of energy. The Chinese are now working on a deepwater port and industrial park, also in Rakhine state, that will serve as a critical node in its one-belt, one-road project. Reports indicate that with regard to the park, in fact, state-owned China's CITIC Group is seeking an extraordinary 85 percent stake in exchange for taking a loss on the suspended Myitsone dam project.[3]

---

[1] Namrata Goswami, "Tracking the source of 'Weapon Providers' for NE Rebels," IDSA Comment, November 07, 2013, http://www.idsa.in/idsacomments/TrackingthesourceofWeaponProvidersforNERebels_ngoswami_071113 (accessed on September 26, 2017).

[2] Lawi Weng, "AK-47's – Made in Wa State," *The Irrawaddy*, December 16, 2008 http://www2.irrawaddy.com/article.php?art_id=14804 (accessed on September 26, 2017).

[3] Yimou Lee and Shwe Yee Saw Myint, "Exclusive: China Seeks up to 85 Percent Stake in Strategic Port in Myanmar," Reuters, May 05, 2017, http://www.reuters.com/article/us-china-silkroad-myanmar-port-exclusive/exclusive-china-seeks-up-to-85-percent-stake-in-strategic-port-in-myanmar-idUSKBN1811DF (accessed on September 26, 2017).

The bottom line is that the Chinese are not about to stand by and watch relationships that have secured this position compromised by other outside powers. Neither will Beijing be critical of Burmese security operations in the very location of its investments.

Beijing essentially play both sides of the fence in Burma. From 1989, when both Burma and China were facing a difficult international environment, their militaries became very close. The Burmese were facing isolation for the crackdown on pro-democracy demonstrators and the arrest of Aung San Suu Kyi and China for the Tiananmen Square massacre. Chinese military assistance to Burma in the years following this marriage of convenience is estimated at $2 billion. This was a level of engagement that "helped transform the Myanmar military from a 'small, weak counter-insurgency force' into a 'powerful defence force capable of major conventional operations.'"[4] And they continue today as the "single largest source of equipment and training for Burma's military forces."[5]

So, at the same time that the Chinese are receiving State Counsellor Aung San Suu Kyi in Beijing and facilitating her efforts to reach cease-fire arrangements with Burma's EAGs, they materially support some of the most well-armed among them as well as support her rivals for power in the Burmese military. Yes, by all accounts, the Burmese military has problems with China. For decades it contended with a China-supported communist insurgency. The military distrusts the Chinese and wants to lessen their reliance on them. And yes, this was a factor in Burma's decision to open up to the West, including to the United States. But in the geopolitical game, the Chinese have a team on the field, too, and it has a great deal more to offer than the training workshops that were proposed by the Senate Armed Servicesd Committee earlier this month. For such meager feed, in fact, it is not clear that the Burmese are at all interested in closer ties with the U.S. military.

Reform Political Dynamic

The second misjudgment embedded in the pursuit of closer mil-to-mil relations is the thinking that through engagement with the military, the U.S. has the ability to significantly impact the Burmese political dynamic in favor of reform. As is well-known, the 2008 constitution gives civilian authorities in Burma no control over the military or the portfolios—defense, border affairs, and home affairs—that they hold in the cabinet. The theory, as I have heard expressed many times by proponents of closer mil-to-mil ties is that, given this, the U.S. should to induce the military to cooperate in reforms by giving it the direct benefit of a relationship with the U.S. military. The concern is that otherwise it will have no stake in democratic reforms, and will, therefore, be of a mind to subvert them.

Setting aside that the most plausible leverage in this regard were the prohibitions on doing business with military-linked businesses that were lifted at the end of Obama's term, this theory ignores the equities that the military has in not fully cooperating with future reforms. The Burmese military had its own objectives for initiating the reforms under the previous regime, objectives that did not encompass fundamental reform of its own sources of power.

---

[4] Ian Storey, *Southeast Asia and the Rise of China: The Search for Security* (London: Routledge, February 2013).

[5] Priscilla A. Clapp, "China's Relations with Burma," testimony before the U.S.–China Economic and Security Review Commission on China's Relations with Southeast Asia, May 13, 2015, https://www.usip.org/publications/2015/05/chinas-relations-burma (accessed on September 26, 2017).

So much has happened in Burma over the past six years. The military relinquished formal power over large swaths of the government. Political prisoners have been freed; restrictions on the press and assembly have eased; a national human rights commission has been established. The political environment has become competitive. Most significantly, democracy icon Aung San Suu Kyi was released from house arrest and allowed to organize politically. She led her party to victory in 2015 parliamentary elections, and in 2016 assumed power over the civilian government. However, Burma's human rights situation has remained challenging even with these changes. Although a far cry from the more than 2,000 political prisoners held in the pre-reform era, 98 people remain in jail serving sentences or awaiting trial for political crimes. And arrests continue—38 in the month of August alone.[6] Human Rights Watch characterizes the situation as follows in its 2017 World Report: "Restrictions on the rights to freedom of expression and assembly persist, amid the government's failure to contend with the range of rights-abusing laws that have been long used to criminalize free speech and prosecute dissidents."[7] Freedom House still classifies Burma's press environment as "not free,"[8] with a score worse than Cambodia. Again, Burma is much better off in regard to both press freedom and broader political freedoms than it was in 2010, but stalled in terms of forward progress.

The United States and other states in the international community can continue trying to chip away at these lingering issues, but the fundamental political reforms that are needed involve curbing the political power of the military. The grants of power given it by the 2008 constitution, guarantee of 25 percent of seats in parliament that enable it to veto any amendments, control over the three aforementioned ministries, "control over its own judicial processes, including when allegations of human rights violations are involved,"[9] and extraordinary powers to reassert control in the event of an emergency—these all remain obstacles to fuller political reform and imbue the military with a sense of impunity.

By many accounts, the transition from military to civilian government that culminated in the 2015 election was meticulously planned. The military government's 2003 "Roadmap to Democracy" was intended to get it to where it is today, not farther. Its freeing of Aung San Suu Kyi, as renowned Burma expert Bertil Lintner, who has reviewed internal documents related to the roadmap, says, was part of an effort to ease its opening to the West, no more, no less. Ultimately, he says, these documents are clear: The ultimate aim of the military is to "crush" the opposition.[10] The military has power, it has a plan, and it is not going to bargain it away in exchange for a relationship with the U.S. military.

Nature of the Burmese Military

The third misjudgment in the pursuit of closer U.S.–Burma military-to-military relations involves the character of the Burmese military. Beyond the strategic decision it has made to share

---

[6] Political Prisoner Data, Assistance Association for Political Prisoners (Burma), http://aappb.org/political-prisoner-data/ (accessed September 26, 2017)

[7] Human Rights Watch, "World Report 2017: Burma," (accessed on September 26, 2017), https://www.hrw.org/world-report/2017/country-chapters/burmaBurma (accessed on September 26, 2017).

[8] Freedom House, "Myanmar Country Report: Freedom of the Press 2017," (accessed on September 26, 2017), https://freedomhouse.org/report/freedom-press/2017/myanmarMyanmar (accessed on September 26, 2017).

[9] Amnesty International, "Myanmar 2016/2017," (accessed on September 26, 2017), https://www.amnesty.org/en/countries/asia-and-the-pacific/myanmar/report-myanmar/ (accessed on September 26, 2017).

[10] Bertil Lintner, "The People's Republic of China and Burma," Project 2049 Institute, May 9, 2017, http://www.project2049.net/documents/China_Burma_Lintner_Pauk_Phaw2049.pdf (accessed on September 26, 2017).

responsibilities with an elected civilian government, what has changed about the military that makes it a more palatable partner today than it has been in the past? In fact, there should be nothing surprising about its recent offensive against the Rohingya. This "text book example of ethnic cleansing"[11] has a decades-long history rooted in military governments' denial of Rohingya rights commensurate with citizenship. The persecution reached its most recent previous climax in 2012. At a time when intercommunal violence between Muslims and Buddhists were flaring, Burmese security forces in Rakhine were documented working with extremist groups there to drive the Rohingya out of the country.[12]

In short, the images of people, wretched and fleeing Rakhine by sea or river crossings, is nothing new. And its treatment of the Rohingya is in keeping with the military's behavior in other areas. The State Department's most recent report on Burma's human rights situation testifies to the continued fear that security forces exert in conflict areas more generally "through physical abuse and threats to individual livelihoods." "Public information was unavailable as to the results of any military investigations into such abuses," it says, "and generally security forces appeared to act with impunity."[13]

This is essentially the same Burmese military today that it was prior to 2011. With so little upside to dealing with it, as explained above, the downside of associating with such characters carries only downsides.

Conclusion and Recommendations

One thing I hope Congress will take stock of as it addresses concerns about the current situation in Rakhine state and America's approach to Burma more generally is its own history of leadership. For 20 years, Congress led on Burma policy. It established the laws—the 1997 investment ban, the 2003 Burma Freedom and Democracy Act, the 2008 Jade Act—that governed our policy. The extraordinarily complex set of overlapping authorities created by these laws and past Presidents' executive orders were not the neatest way of addressing the problems in Burma. But they were responsive. They were responsive to developments on the ground in Burma and they were responsive to core American values. It should take leadership again. Burma has changed. The situation there, including in Rakhine, requires a fresh look. Congress should enact comprehensive legislation that reconciles these realities by setting new goals and the best ways of going about addressing them. The Heritage Foundation's Asian Studies Center is currently engaged in a project to demonstrate what exactly this might look like. Some of its preliminary proposals are as follows:

- **Refrain from further normalization of military-to-military relations with Burma.** Senator John McCain's (R–AZ) decision to remove provisions of the 2018 National Defense Authorization Act (NDAA) granting the Department of Defense authority to provide the

[11] Annie Gowen, "'Textbook Example of Ethnic Cleansing': 370,000 Rohingyas Flood Bangladesh as Crisis Worsens," *The Washington Post*, September 12, 2017, https://www.washingtonpost.com/world/textbook-example-of-ethnic-cleansing--370000-rohingyas-flood-bangladesh-as-crisis-worsens/2017/09/12/24b[290e-8792-41e9-a769-c79d7326bed0_story.html?utm_term=.bced0e5f00ca (accessed on September 26, 2017).

[12] Stuart Leavenworth, "'Yale Study Accuses Myanmar of Genocide against Muslim Minority," McClatchy DC Bureau, October 29, 2015, http://www.mcclatchydc.com/news/nation-world/world/article41822457.html (accessed on September 26, 2017).

[13] U.S. Department of State, Bureau of Democracy, Human Rights and Labor, *Burma 2016 Human Rights Report*, 2016, https://www.state.gov/documents/organization/265536.pdf (accessed on September 26, 2017).

Burmese military consultation, education, and training was a step in the right direction.[14] Congress should go further and rescind the authorities granted in the 2015 NDAA that laid the groundwork for them.

- **Codify the embargo on the export of defense articles and services to Burma that dates to 1993.** Codifying the embargo will make any relaxation of it subject to extensive consultations with Congress and require its explicit agreement.
- **Re-impose restrictions on Americans doing business** with military-linked companies and procurement/contracting entities.[15]
- **Continue the prohibition** on International Military Education and Training (IMET) and Foreign Military (FMF) assistance to Burma.
- **Re-impose asset freezes and visa bans on the Burmese military** and give these measures basis in new U.S. law tied to new policy goals.
- **Establish policy goals** to include a cessation of abuse against unarmed civilians in Rakhine state and other conflict zones; access to conflict zones by journalists, humanitarian groups, and international fact-finding missions; establish an environment conducive to the return of refugees; and verified cessation of military ties to North Korea.

Even in the midst of the crisis in Rakhine state, there will be objections to Congress taking a hard line on the U.S. relationship with the Burmese military. They will argue that it will take us out of the great geopolitical game vis-à-vis China. They will argue that the Burmese military needs to be given a stake in reform if it is to continue. Those arguments, as demonstrated, are specious. The stronger argument will cast doubt on the efficacy of new sanctions in furthering reform and bringing about change in the military. Indeed, it is difficult to translate pressure into transformation. It is extremely difficult to force a military like Burma's unrestrained by civilian authority to concede what it has determined is in the interest of its institution. In acting, however, Congress can give a modicum of leverage to democratic forces in Burma. And it can put the U.S. on the right side. This is not an opportunity we have in every country in the region. Each case requires an approach tailored to its circumstances. But in Burma, given factors of geography, domestic dynamics, and history, the U.S. should press home its values.

---

[14] News Release, "SASC Chairman John McCain Seeks to Remove Burma Military Cooperation from NDAA," Office of Senator John McCain, September 12, 2017, https://www.mccain.senate.gov/public/index.cfm/2017/9/sasc-chairman-john-mccain-seeks-to-remove-burma-military-cooperation-from-ndaa (accessed on September 26, 2017).

[15] Steptoe International, "U.S. Lifts All Economic Sanctions on Myanmar (Burma)," Steptoe International Compliance Blog, October 7, 2016, (accessed on September 26, 2017), http://www.steptoeinternationalcomplianceblog.com/2016/10/u-s-lifts-all-economic-sanctions-on-myanmar-burma/ (accessed on September 26, 2017).

* * * * * * * * * * * * * * * * * *

The Heritage Foundation is a public policy, research, and educational organization recognized as exempt under section 501(c)(3) of the Internal Revenue Code. It is privately supported and receives no funds from any government at any level, nor does it perform any government or other contract work.

The Heritage Foundation is the most broadly supported think tank in the United States. During 2016, it had hundreds of thousands of individual, foundation, and corporate supporters representing every state in the U.S. Its 2016 income came from the following sources:

Individuals 75.3%
Foundations 20.3%
Corporations 1.8%
Program revenue and other income 2.6%

The top five corporate givers provided The Heritage Foundation with 1.0% of its 2016 income. The Heritage Foundation's books are audited annually by the national accounting firm of RSM US, LLP.

Mr. YOHO. Mr. Lohman, I appreciate it.

Mr. Sullivan, if you would go ahead. Thank you.

STATEMENT OF MR. DANIEL P. SULLIVAN, SENIOR ADVOCATE FOR HUMAN RIGHTS, REFUGEES INTERNATIONAL

Mr. SULLIVAN. First, I would like to take the opportunity to thank Chairman Royce, Chairman Yoho, and Ranking Member Sherman, and the members of this subcommittee for holding this very timely and very important hearing.

Mr. Chairman, there is a tragedy of historic proportions that is unfolding right now in Myanmar, also known as Burma. Nearly ½ million of one single ethnic group, the Rohingya, have now fled from the country. That is at least one-third of the entire population that was living there up to a month ago. There are now more people, more Rohingya living in Bangladesh than there are in Burma, in Myanmar. Hundreds if not thousands of Rohingya have been killed.

There is no question that crimes against humanity and ethnic cleansing are taking place. I know this is happening because I was there in Bangladesh hearing firsthand from people who had experienced these abuses. Refugees International's president, Eric Schwartz, who is a former White House official and assistant Secretary of State, he has spent three decades, a career in various dozens of humanitarian and human rights missions, told me that this is one of the worst he has ever seen.

I would like just to share one story that I think is illustrative. There is a woman named Lila, a 28-year-old mother of three daughters all under the age of seven. She told me how just a few days before she had been in her village in Rakhine state when soldiers, Myanmar soldiers came and surrounded her village, lit their homes on fire, shot at them. They fled. One of the soldiers grabbed her by the arm and tried to drag her away. She somehow escaped. Her husband told them to go ahead without him. He was going to try to get the family cows and bring them over. She with her three young daughters went by foot over the border to Bangladesh hiding in waist-deep water for long periods of time and arrived with just the clothes on her back. Just a few days later, she heard from neighbors who arrived that they had found her husband's body in the river with a gunshot wound to the back of the head. This is just one of so many stories that I and so many others have heard from people fleeing.

It is important to recognize ARSA, and it is important to recognize that there are other minorities, Rakhine Buddhists and Hindus who have been killed and displaced, but it is nowhere near on the scale of the Rohingya.

The response of the Myanmar military has been grossly disproportional. It has also unleashed a humanitarian tragedy and crisis in Bangladesh. The Government of Bangladesh, to its great credit, has largely welcomed the Rohingya. It will be vital for the government to continue to work with international agencies, the UNHCR, the International Organization for Migration, and international NGOs to address the needs. I would just highlight the need for psychosocial and other services for gender-based violence, and the heightened risk of human trafficking.

The announcement of $32 million in U.S. aid was a very welcome shot in the arm, but U.N. agencies are now reporting there will be at least $200 million needed over the next 6 months to address the crisis.

In the interest of time, I am happy to speak further on the humanitarian situation with the question period. But ultimately, the only true long-term solution is to address the root causes, and I would just like to highlight three levels of responsibility.

First and foremost, as we have heard, a name I think we should be hearing more and more is Senior General Min Aung Hlaing and the military. It is the Myanmar soldiers who are at the front lines of committing these abuses, and they are also those with the most power to bring them to an end.

Secondly, there is the civilian leadership in Aung San Suu Kyi. She has not simply been silent; she has refused to allow a U.N. factfinding mission to come in. Her office has accused international NGOs of supporting terrorism. In her first address on the crisis to the world last week, she expressed ignorance as to why people were fleeing in such numbers, and indicated that the fact that less than 50 percent of the villages being burned was, by her account, was somehow okay.

Yes, she is limited in her influence by the military, but she still has a strong voice. And so far, she has only used it largely just to defend actions that are patently indefensible.

The third level of responsibility is with world leaders, and in the context of this hearing, with the U.S. Government. I thank Members of Congress and members of this subcommittee for speaking out on the Rohingya, but so much more is needed.

There are several steps that the U.S. Congress can take, and I just quickly highlight a few. Prohibiting military to military cooperation with Myanmar; placing targeted sanctions on Senior General Min Aung Hlaing and other senior leaders, as well as military-owned enterprises; urging the Trump administration to list those individuals on the Specially Designated Nationals list; also, pressing the Trump administration to work through the U.N. Security Council for multilateral measures, including an arms embargo, targeted sanctions, and authorization of collecting of evidence and possible referral to the ICC if accountability is not had.

I would also emphasize support for robust humanitarian efforts in Bangladesh and the need to push for humanitarian access within Myanmar. Ultimately, for long-term solutions the Kofi Annan advisory commission recommendations should be implemented.

Allow me to end on just a personal reflection that when I first started hearing the accounts of what was happening, getting videos from credible sources and seeing the masses moving to the border, I knew this was something different, and it had shades of Darfur, Srebrenica, and Rwanda. I hope that we are not looking back in the same way and asking what more could we have done to prevent the Rohingya going down that same road. Thank you.

[The prepared statement of Mr. Sullivan follows:]

REFUGEES INTERNATIONAL

Testimony of Daniel P. Sullivan
Senior Advocate for Human Rights
Refugees International
House Committee on Foreign Affairs
Subcommittee on Asia and the Pacific
"Burma's Brutal Campaign Against the Rohingya"
September 27, 2017

I would like to take this opportunity to thank Chairman Yoho, Ranking Member Sherman and the members of this subcommittee for holding this timely hearing today, and I ask that my full statement and additional Refugees International (RI) documents be ordered part of the record. RI is a non-profit, non-governmental organization that advocates for lifesaving assistance and protection for displaced people in parts of the world impacted by conflict, persecution and forced displacement. Based here in Washington, we conduct fact-finding missions to research and report on the circumstances of displaced populations in countries such as Somalia, Iraq, Uganda, and Bangladesh. RI does not accept any government or United Nations funding, which helps ensure that our advocacy is impartial and independent.

Chairman Yoho, Ranking Member Sherman, today's important hearing could not come at a more crucial time. There is a tragedy of historic proportions unfolding at this moment in Myanmar. More than four hundred thousand people of a single ethnic group, the Rohingya, have fled Myanmar for Bangladesh in less than a month. That is more than one-third of the total number of Rohingya that were living in the country up to a month ago.

The Myanmar military continues to relentlessly attack Rohingya villages, burning homes, beating, stabbing, and shooting the inhabitants, and leading survivors to flee for their lives. Doctors and humanitarian workers have reported widespread cases of rape. Hundreds, if not thousands of Rohingya, have been killed.

There is no question that crimes against humanity and ethnic cleansing are taking place. This was obvious three weeks ago, when RI first publicly accused the Myanmar military of such atrocities.

I know this is happening because I heard the stories myself. Only a few days ago, I returned from visiting Bangladesh to speak with Rohingya who recently fled to ask them why. What I heard was a litany of abuses along a common strain: soldiers surrounding villages, using various incendiary devices to set fire to homes, at times locking or throwing people inside the burning structures; young women singled out to be taken away and raped; days long flight by foot and/or boat across the border to Bangladesh, arriving with just the clothes on their backs.

RI's president, Eric Schwartz, a former White House official and Assistant Secretary of State for Populations, Refugees, and Migration, traveled with me to Bangladesh to meet the newly arrived Rohingya. Together we visited several camps and a hospital where we saw young girls and boys who had suffered gunshot wounds, burns, and physical injuries and emotional trauma inflicted by the Myanmar military. Eric has said that, over a three decade career, he's been on dozens of humanitarian and human rights missions, but doesn't remember choking up on any of them – until this particular trip. The situation, he told me, is one of the worst he's ever seen. I can only concur.

I thank Members of Congress, including Members of this Committee, for speaking out on behalf of the Rohingya. But mere words are no longer sufficient, Mr. Chairman. The time for action is now, and I will lay out in my testimony what action Congress should take immediately.

Background

My testimony today is based on my recent first-hand conversations with Rohingya in Bangladesh and years of working on the Rohingya, including visits to Malaysia, Thailand, Bangladesh, and Rakhine State in Myanmar. Past RI reports have documented the persecution faced by the Rohingya as a stateless group. They have described how the Rohingya have been refused citizenship by the Myanmar government despite historical claims to the country going back generations. And RI reports have described the severe restrictions on basic freedoms to marry, have children, practice religion, work, or to move freely. The Rohingya have even been denied the right to self-identify, as the Myanmar government refuses to recognize "Rohingya" as a distinct ethnic group.

The current crisis is the horrific culmination of these decades of persecution and more recent troubling developments. Even as the much lauded democratic opening of the past few years unfolded in Myanmar, conditions for the Rohingya were getting worse. Since violence between Rohingya and local Rakhine Buddhists broke out in 2012, some 120,000 Rohingya have remained confined to displacement camps described as 'open air prisons'. Tens of thousands took to sea to escape conditions in Myanmar, leading to the May 2015 Andaman Sea crisis that briefly captured the world's attention as thousands of Rohingya and Bangladeshis were abandoned on rickety boats by human traffickers.

The prevailing conditions were noted in a report by an international advisory commission on Rakhine State, led by former UN Secretary General Kofi Annan (one appointed and endorsed by Aung San Suu Kyi). It found that the Rohingya population has suffered "protracted statelessness and profound discrimination" that has caused the Rohingya community to become "marginalized and particularly vulnerable." It noted that several aspects of Myanmar's citizenship law "are not in compliance with international standards and norms" and that the citizenship law "has not done justice to the credible claims of communities who have been living in the country for generations." The report's recommendations included the need for unfettered humanitarian access, safe returns of refugees, and an "independent and impartial investigation" to ensure "that perpetrators of serious human rights violations are held accountable." It was even accepted by Aung San Suu Kyi and the Myanmar military, but any hoped for progress it might provide has been quickly overshadowed.

Starting late last year the situation took a decided turn for the worse. In October 2016, an insurgent group of Rohingya calling itself the Arakan Rohingya Salvation Army (ARSA), emerged publicly with an attack on border guard posts that left nine police officers dead. The insurgents attacked largely with knives and sling shots and some firearms. The response by the Myanmar military was grossly disproportional, targeting the entire Rohingya population, and indiscriminately wreaking severe human rights abuses upon them, including torture, arbitrary execution, and mass rape. Some 87,000 Rohingya would flee to Bangladesh in the next few months. The Office of the High Commissioner for Human Rights carried out interviews with Rohingya who fled to Bangladesh and concluded that abuses were occurring that likely amounted to crimes against humanity. The UN Human Rights Council then established a Fact-Finding Mission to investigate further, but the Government of Myanmar said it would not cooperate or allow investigators access to the country.

RI's most recent report, in July 2017, documented the experience of some of the 87,000 Rohingya who fled to Bangladesh at that time and the serious humanitarian challenges that influx brought to Bangladesh. Among the challenges highlighted by RI were inadequate shelter, unequal and inefficient aid distribution, and the rising risks of gender based violence and human trafficking. All of this was before August 25th, before the population of Rohingya in the country effectively doubled in the course of a month.

The current crisis began on August 25th, a day after the Annan Commission report was released, when new attacks by ARSA on some 30 police posts led to a wildly disproportionate military response against the broader Rohingya civilian population. Like ARSA's October attacks, ARSA's August attacks were carried out largely with knives, sticks, and home-made weapons. Twelve police officers were killed, along with dozens of insurgents, according to the Myanmar government.

It is important to recognize that other minority groups in Rakhine State, including Rakhine Buddhists and Hindus, have also been displaced and killed, many reportedly by ARSA insurgents, but nowhere on the scale of the Rohingya. As I mentioned at the beginning of this testimony, more than 400,000 of the just over a million Rohingya living in Myanmar as of last month have now been displaced. Hundreds, if not thousands, have been killed. It is difficult to get a completely accurate picture as access to Rakhine State remains heavily restricted. But speaking with those who have fled provides us with a very good idea of what is happening in the region.

Fleeing Horrors in Myanmar

The story of one woman I spoke with, Lila, is similar – in some ways, nearly identical – to other accounts I obtained. Lila, a 28-year-old mother of three daughters, all under the age of seven, was in her village in Boli Bazar in Maungdaw district of Rakhine State in western Myanmar just a matter of days ago. Soldiers came to her village and began lighting the houses on fire. One soldier grabbed her by the arm and tried to drag her away but somehow she managed to escape. After she escaped the burning village, her husband told her to go ahead with her three daughters without him while he went to fetch the family's cows and try to bring them along. He told her he would catch up with her in Bangladesh. So she fled across the border hiding for long periods in water with her three small girls until she reached the sprawling and rapidly emerging makeshift shelters in Bangladesh. But a few days after Lila arrived in Bangladesh, neighbors arrived with the news that her husband's body had been found in a river, with a gunshot wound through the back of his head.

It was an account all too familiar to the Rohingya with whom I spoke in Bangladesh. Numerous similar accounts have been collected by groups like Human Rights Watch, Amnesty International, and Fortify Rights. The Arakan Project, a group with a network of monitors throughout Rakhine State has described the attacks as systematic. Sometimes it is soldiers destroying the villages. Sometimes it is local ethnic Rakhine vigilantes setting the fires. And other times it is a mix of the two. Satellite images show clear patterns of destruction, vast swaths of burned villages in line with the accounts repeatedly told by Rohingya refugees; Rohingya neighborhoods burned to the ground while nearby non-Rohingya neighborhoods remain untouched. The Myanmar government claims the fires were started by the Rohingya themselves, but provides no proof. It also refuses access to any outside observers, most notably the fact-finding mission established by the UN Human Rights Council to investigate similar abuses widely reported in the last months of 2016, begging the question of what they are trying to hide.

The Border Guard Patrol across the border in Bangladesh has described hearing and seeing what they determined to be mortar fire in areas where fleeing civilians had congregated. The Government of Bangladesh has lodged official complaints about the laying of land mines along the Myanmar side of the border. And we've received credible reports that those land mines are being laid further inside the country around Rohingya villages.

What the hundreds of thousands of Rohingya fleeing to Bangladesh describe are no less than crimes against humanity perpetrated by a military already with a troubling track record. And the UN High Commissioner for Human Rights came to the clear conclusion that what is unfolding "seems to be a textbook example of ethnic cleansing." We certainly agree.

A Humanitarian Crisis in Bangladesh

The actions of the Myanmar military have also created a humanitarian crisis as aid efforts in Bangladesh, which was already home to 300,000 to 500,000 Rohingya who had fled past bouts of violence and persecution, have been quickly overwhelmed. When I visited Bangladesh a few months ago, the government and international agencies were still grappling with the influx of some 87,000 Rohingya from attacks that had taken place over the last months of 2016, including makeshift settlements of tens of thousands that popped up in the course of a week.

On my most recent visit, which ended last week, the explosion of refugees was startling. Masses of people lined the roads in and around new makeshift settlements popping up in real time. Women and children dragged bamboo poles and tarps, wading through ankle deep mud to build new shelters. Hills and swaths of land that had been completely green were stripped and overrun by new arrivals, desperate for some kind of shelter from the steady rains of the monsoon season after days fleeing on foot.

The government of Bangladesh, to its great credit, has taken an overall welcoming stance. The government has announced plans to build more than 14,000 shelters on 2,000 acres of land. It has begun to register new arrivals and provide biometric identity cards, with technical assistance provided by the UN Refugee Agency (UNHCR). Serious concerns with implementation of plans, both in terms of building of adequate structures and providing freedom of movement remain and must be addressed, but in its overall response to such a crisis Bangladesh has been on the right side of history. It will be vital that the government work with international agencies, including UNHCR, the International Organization for Migration (IOM), and international NGOs to ensure proper coordination, building of shelter according to global best practices, and adequate provision of not only food, sanitation, and medical care, but also psychosocial and other support specific to victims of gender based violence. I would also like to highlight that in RI's previous report we noted the heightened risks of human trafficking cited by several humanitarian officials. With the new influx, those risks will only be further heightened.

The needs are overwhelming. The support and solidarity of the global community is sorely needed. The announcement of $32 million in humanitarian aid by the United States was a welcome shot in the arm, but much more is needed. IOM has released a flash appeal for $26.1 million as part of a gap of $77 million identified as needed through the end of this year by the Inter Sector Coordination Group, the coalition of agencies coordinating the humanitarian response in Bangladesh. UN High Commissioner for Refugees Filippo Grandi just visited the makeshift camps for Rohingya in Bangladesh, and has stated that UNHCR will need $200 million for the next 6 months to address the humanitarian crisis.

And this is before mentioning the hundreds of thousands of Rohingya remaining inside Rakhine State, many blocked off from any kind of aid. Even before the attacks started, UNICEF was estimating 80,000 children under the age of five were facing acute malnutrition.

Addressing the Root Causes

Ultimately, the only true solution to the enduring misery of more than 400,000 Rohingya people in Bangladesh is addressing the root causes of their flight, the actions of the military in Myanmar.

The only way to address the root causes is to address the actions of those bearing greatest responsibility. So I would like to take a moment to discuss the actions and roles of the Myanmar military, civilian leader Aung San Suu Kyi, and the international community.

First and foremost, the Myanmar military led by Senior General Min Aung Laing is directly responsible for this crisis. It is Myanmar soldiers and their leadership who are both the primary actors in perpetrating serious human rights abuses taking place and those in the strongest position to bring them to an end. As described earlier, there are numerous eye witness accounts from Rohingya who have fled to Bangladesh identifying men in Myanmar army uniforms attacking their villages, burning their homes, and stabbing or shooting their loved ones. These accounts are fortified by video and satellite evidence and the accounts of Bangladesh Border Guards observing fleeing masses, gunfire, and burning villages from across the border. The Myanmar military continues to refuse to allow outside access to areas of Rakhine State affected by the violence.

A second level of responsibility lies with the civilian leadership of Myanmar, with Aung San Suu Kyi as its *de facto* head. A lot has been said about the limits she faces with a military that continues to wield enormous influence in the country, controlling much of the economy, guaranteed 25 percent of parliamentary seats under a constitution they crafted, and with primary authority over the security operations taking place. Much has also been said about the anti-Rohingya sentiments that pervade the vast majority of the population in Myanmar, making it a politically tenuous position to speak out about the rights of the Rohingya. All that is true. But it must also be recognized that Suu Kyi is not powerless. She has a prominent voice in the international community and among the domestic masses that overwhelmingly supported her in the last elections.

Mr. Chairman, I do not need to remind you and your colleagues in Congress about the enormous efforts the U.S. Congress has undertaken on behalf of Suu Kyi, when she languished under house arrest or when she was attacked while campaigning. Under the leadership of the late Tom Lantos, the distinguished former Chairman of this Foreign Affairs Committee, the United States Congress imposed comprehensive sanctions against the previous military regime, in support of the very National League for Democracy (NLD) leaders who are in power today. Suu Kyi was even awarded the Congressional Medal of Honor. Yet, many of her supporters are asking where her voice is today on the abuse of the Rohingya.

Yet, she has not simply been silent. She has rejected the UN fact-finding mission, and said or allowed those representing her to spread dangerous and unfounded allegations that have served to stoke tensions. For example, when World Food Programme nutrition biscuits were found in insurgent camps, Suu Kyi's office posted photos citing it as evidence that international NGOs are supporting terrorism, a baseless allegation that has endangered international aid workers trying to supply lifesaving assistance to those most in need. Just a few days ago an aid truck of the International Federation of the Red Cross was attacked by an angry crowd of Rakhine villagers.

In her first address to the world on the Rohingya crisis on September 19th, Suu Kyi expressed ignorance as to why at least a third of the entire Rohingya population of Myanmar fled within the span of just three weeks, made no mention of credible reports of massive violations of human rights against the Rohingya community, and asserted that all people in Rakhine state have access to education and healthcare services without discrimination. She further declared that "[m]ore than 50 percent of the villages of Muslims are intact" as if destruction of Rohingya villages was somehow acceptable as long as the level was less than 50 percent. Yes, Aung San Suu Kyi's power is constrained, but she is not without a voice, and so far, that voice has largely served to defend actions that are patently indefensible.

The third level of responsibility is that of the international community, specifically its political leaders, and in the particular context of this hearing, the responsibility of the United States government to speak out and act. As the crisis has worsened, more world leaders have been speaking out. In remarks to the Security Council on Wednesday of last week, Vice President Pence stated that "President Trump and I…call on this Security Council and the United Nations to take strong and swift action to bring this crisis to an end and give hope and hep to the Rohingya people in their hour of need." Although this came more than three weeks after the crisis began, it was a welcome statement. But it will be largely meaningless if not followed by vigorous action on the part of U.S. officials.

As reflected by today's hearing, there has also been congressional interest in this tragedy, and I note that draft language in the Senate that provided for expanded military to military relations between the United States and Myanmar has been effectively scrapped.

But the actions that have been taken thus far are wholly inadequate, and much more pressure is needed to put an end to the ongoing violence.

There are several steps the U.S. Congress can and should take to address the ongoing tragedy.

The Congress should:

- Prohibit military to military cooperation with Myanmar until abuses are ended and individuals involved in planning, aiding or carrying out such abuses against the Rohingya are held accountable.
- Place targeted sanctions on Senior General Min Aung Hlaing and other senior military officials and military-owned enterprises and urge the Trump Administration to list them on the Specially Designated Nationals (SDN) list until the gross human rights abuses taking place are brought to an end and those responsible are held accountable.
- Press the Trump Administration to work through the UN Security Council toward open debate on the Rohingya crisis in Myanmar with a strong statement calling for cessation of abuses, access for the fact-finding mission, and imposition of measures with real consequences including:
  - Targeted sanctions on Senior General Min Aung Hlaing and other senior military officials and military-owned enterprises;
  - A multilateral arms embargo on Myanmar;
  - Authorization of evidence collection toward holding accountable those responsible for gross human rights abuses.
  - Support for a referral to the International Criminal Court unless the Myanmar authorities take significant measures to address the human rights concerns and to hold accountable those responsible for gross human rights abuses.
- Demand unfettered international humanitarian access to Rakhine State.
- Support robust humanitarian aid efforts in Bangladesh in the near term with the aim for eventual safe and voluntary return of Rohingya to Myanmar.
- For long term solutions, endorse and push for progress on the recommendations of the Advisory Commission on Rakhine State led by former UN Secretary General Kofi Annan.

Critics of an approach involving sanctions may warn that such actions will endanger Aung San Suu Kyi's efforts to build toward a democratic transition, or may prompt the military to take more drastic measures against the civilian government or against the Rohingya community. It is true that sanctions must be used carefully and cautiously to avoid unintended consequences. It is also true that sanctions are no silver bullet. Nonetheless, RI strongly believes that they are a necessary part of an effective response to the current horrors. The alternative is to stand aside while ethnic cleansing and crimes against humanity unfold. Already one third of the Rohingya population has been forcibly displaced from their homes in Myanmar. If the estimates amid the chaotic exodus are correct, there are now more Rohingya in Bangladesh than there are remaining in Myanmar. How bad does it have to get?

Allow me to end with a personal reflection. When I started getting desperate warnings that something new and disastrous was unfolding, when I started receiving horrific videos taken by credible sources, and heard of the desperate masses descending on the Bangladesh border, I couldn't help but feel shades of Rwanda, Bosnia, and Darfur. Before 1994, hardly anyone knew where Rwanda was. Before 1995, hardly anyone had heard of Srebrenica. Before 2004, hardly anyone had heard of Darfur. The more this plays out, the more I fear that is exactly the road we are going down. Years later we all look back at those tragedies and wonder what could have been done to prevent them. Let's not allow the treatment of the Rohingya to become the Rwanda, Srebrenica, or Darfur we all look back upon with the same question.

Mr. YOHO. Mr. Sullivan, I appreciate your testimony. I read it, and I could tell it was laced with a lot of emotion, and I can tell that by your testimony, and I appreciate you being here and reporting to us.

Ms. Gittleman, if you would be so kind.

STATEMENT OF MS. ANDREA GITTLEMAN, PROGRAM MANAGER, SIMON-SKJODT CENTER FOR THE PREVENTION OF GENOCIDE, U.S. HOLOCAUST MEMORIAL MUSEUM

Ms. GITTLEMAN. Thank you, Chairman Yoho and Ranking Member Sherman, for convening this hearing on such an urgent matter.

I speak on behalf of the United States Holocaust Memorial Museum, Simon-Skjodt Center for the Prevention of Genocide. We draw upon lessons learned from the Holocaust, and the failure to prevent genocide then, in order to inform policy decisions today. It is with great alarm that we are here to discuss yet another situation of mass atrocity that the world is failing to prevent and local authorities are refraining from halting.

The Simon-Skjodt Center sounded the alarm about early warning signs of genocide against the Rohingya 2 years ago. Even then, the warning signs were clear, including the denial of citizenship, segregation between Rohingya Muslims and Buddhist Rakhine, and impunity for violence against Rohingya. In fact, Burma had been listed as one of the top three countries most likely to experience a state-led mass killing in the Museum's early warning project, and that has been every year since the project began. These warning signs were known, yet not heeded by leaders within Burma and others around the world.

During a recent period of renewed international engagement, the Burmese Government perpetuated an enabling environment for mass atrocities. Over the past year, the Simon-Skjodt Center worked with the human rights organization Fortify Rights to gather testimony from Rohingya who have fled northern Rakhine states.

As discussed, deadly attacks by a group known as ARSA were followed by the Burmese military so-called clearance operations, operations that the government stated were to address the threat of militants, but in practice, were brutal and disproportionate attacks against Rohingya civilians. Those who survived shared stories that consistently described the brutality of the Burmese military and their associates, how they attack entire villages and kill men, women, and children, and employ barbaric tactics such as rape and torture under the guise of countering militants.

I spoke to Rohingya refugees in Bangladesh earlier this year after the first round of these so-called clearance operations, and people shared with me horrific stories of witnessing soldiers murder their family members, of fleeing for their lives not knowing of the fate of their loved ones. Women shared disturbing details of sexual violence that appears to have been systematically perpetrated.

While the threat posed by ARSA and any militant group should be taken seriously, the greatest risk to civilians in Rakhine state today is coming from the Burmese military. We are witnessing the commission of crimes against humanity and ethnic cleansing on a horrific scale. Without an immediate end to atrocity crimes and the creation of safe conditions so that those displaced can safely and voluntarily return in the future, we will witness a brutally effective campaign to rid all Rohingya from Burma.

There is mounting evidence that genocide is happening in Burma. There needs to be additional investigation on the intent of perpetrators in order to make a definitive legal declaration of genocide. The Burmese Government is currently blocking efforts to investigate those crimes, but the U.S. has the ability to support such an investigation in order to bring the full truth to light.

While investigations should, of course, move forward, by the time an investigation can be made into genocidal intent, it may be too late. We should not wait for a formal legal finding of genocide before taking action.

The military is the primary perpetrator of mass atrocities and should be pressed with all of our available resources to cease its illegal campaign against Rohingya civilians. While the most urgent demand is for mass atrocities to cease, we must also address the underlying policies and institutions that allowed such crimes to occur.

The ultimate responsibility for deescalating the current cycle of violence and protecting the lives and freedom of Burma's minority populations rests with the country's de facto leader, Aung San Sui Kyi. As a basic principle, we should not fear pressing democratically elected leaders to squarely confront mass atrocities within their country. We can understand the nature of Burma's democratic transitions and the outsized role the military continues to play, while at the same time expecting moral responses from its civilian-led government.

The U.S. Congress does not need to choose between stopping mass atrocities and supporting a democratic government. After all, a democracy in which mass atrocities are occurring is still wholly unacceptable. Thank you.

[The prepared statement of Ms. Gittleman follows:]

Testimony for House Foreign Affairs Committee, Asia and the Pacific Subcommittee: Burma's Brutal Campaign Against the Rohingya

September 27, 2017

Andrea Gittleman, Program Manager, Simon-Skjodt Center for the Prevention of Genocide
U.S. Holocaust Memorial Museum

Thank you, Chairman Yoho and Ranking Member Sherman, for convening this hearing on such an urgent matter. The commission of crimes against humanity and ethnic cleansing, as well as the mounting evidence of genocide by Burma's security forces against the Rohingya minority in Burma demand an immediate response, from both local authorities and the international community. Thank you for pressing for solutions to halt the current atrocities and prevent future ones.

I speak on behalf of the United States Holocaust Memorial Museum's Simon-Skjodt Center for the Prevention of Genocide. We draw upon lessons learned from the Holocaust, and the failure to prevent genocide then, in order to inform policy decisions today. It is with great alarm that we gather here to discuss yet another situation of mass atrocities that the world is failing to prevent and local authorities are refraining from halting.

Failure to Prevent

The Simon-Skjodt Center sounded the alarm about early warning signs of genocide against the Rohingya two years ago, after conducting an on the ground investigation in Rakhine State into state-led acts of persecution and other crimes against humanity that targeted the Rohingya population. Even then, the warning signs were clear – including the denial of citizenship, segregation between Rohingya Muslims and Buddhist Rakhine, and impunity for violence against Rohingya. The Rohingya population has been singled out for restrictions on everyday aspects of daily life, including limitations on freedom of movement that restrict access to health care, education, and the ability to pursue livelihoods. These were all stark warnings of the likelihood of increased targeted violence in the future. In fact, Burma has been listed as one of the top three countries most likely to experience a state-led mass killing in the Museum's early warning project, in every year since the project began.

The warnings signs were known, yet not heeded, by leaders within Burma and others around the world. During this period, governments, including our own, have employed a strategy of engagement, dropping sanctions and other forms of leverage--in the belief that long term democratic change would be the most effective response to the persecution and targeting of Rohingya. However, that engagement has largely occurred without the Burmese government having met clear human rights benchmarks. During this period of renewed international engagement, the Rohingya minority remained subject to state-led persecution and violent attacks. The Burmese government perpetuated an enabling environment for mass atrocities by continuing policies of persecution, failing to hold security forces accountable for past crimes against the Rohingya, and failing to prevent the spread of hate speech. In fact, unchanged policies matched with rising anti-Rohingya sentiment in the country contribute to the risk of further mass killings in Rakhine State not just by the security forces, but by local Rakhine civilians who appear to be increasingly committing crimes against their neighbors. The inclusion of Rakhine civilians in crimes targeting Rohingya is a worrisome development that signals a heightened risk to those Rohingya who remain in northern Rakhine State.

Mass Atrocities

Earlier this year, the Simon-Skjodt Center worked with the Bangkok-based human rights group Fortify Rights to gather testimony from Rohingya who have fled northern Rakhine State in recent weeks. Deadly attacks by a group known as the Arakan Rohingya Salvation Army (ARSA) were followed by the Burmese military's so-called "clearance operations" – operations that the government stated were to address the threat of militants, but in practice were brutal and disproportionate attacks against Rohingya civilians. Those who survived military attacks shared stories that consistently describe the brutality of the Burmese military and their associates, how they attack entire villages and kill men, women, and children, and employ barbaric tactics such as rape and torture, under the guise of countering militants. I spoke to Rohingya refugees in Bangladesh earlier this year after the first round of these "clearance operations," and people shared with me horrific stories of witnessing soldiers murder their family members, of fleeing for their lives not knowing of the fate of their loved ones. While the threat posed by ARSA and any militant group should be taken seriously and not be underestimated, the greatest risk to civilians in Rakhine state today is coming from the Burmese military. The Burmese government has the responsibility to respond to ARSA, but it cannot cast all Rohingya as threats nor respond so disproportionately.

Crimes Against Humanity, Ethnic Cleansing, and Mounting Evidence of Genocide

With estimates of displaced Rohingya over the past year nearing 500,000, which would represent approximately half of the Rohingya population before the so-called "clearance operations," we are witnessing the commission of crimes against humanity and ethnic cleansing on a horrific scale. Without an immediate end to atrocity crimes and the creation of safe conditions so that those displaced can voluntarily return in the future, we will witness a brutally effective campaign to rid all Rohingya from Burma.

There is mounting evidence that genocide is happening in Burma. There needs to be additional investigation on the intent in order to make a definitive legal declaration of genocide. The Burmese government is currently blocking efforts to investigate the crimes. The U.S. has the ability to support such an investigation in order to bring the full truth to light. The U.S. can support an international independent investigation into the mass atrocities against the Rohingya, and it can also commission its own. The U.S. government conducted such an investigation regarding genocide in Sudan, for example, when in 2003 the State Department deployed staff from its Democracy and Human Rights Bureau and its African Affairs Bureau to interview Darfuri refugees in Eastern Chad. These testimonies informed the decision by the Bush Administration to determine the intent of the Sudanese government and to term that violence a genocide.

Though, while investigations should move forward, by the time an investigation can be made into genocidal intent, it may be too late. We should not wait for a formal finding of genocide before taking action.

The Way Forward

The situation before us is complex and dire, and therefore requires a strong response that acknowledges the power structure within Burma. The military is the primary perpetrator of mass atrocities, and should be pressed with all of our available diplomatic resources to cease its illegal campaign against Rohingya civilians. While the most urgent demand is for mass atrocities to cease, we must also address the underlying policies and institutions that allowed such crimes to occur.

There remains a long road ahead of the Burmese people and its government to address the decades of persecution and exclusion that created the conditions for the military to commit these crimes. Burma's leaders should dedicate themselves to the recommendations put forth by the Advisory Commission on Rakhine State, led by former U.N. Secretary-General Kofi Annan, to address the policies and institutions that leave Rohingya so vulnerable to abuse. The Commission's recommendations, including those regarding the restoration of citizenship, freedom of movement, and access to justice should be efficiently adopted. Burma's civilian-led government has the ability to lead on implementing many of those recommendations, and the international community should press Burma's leaders to do so. As Kofi Annan remarked during the issuance of the Commission's final report, addressing these long-standing underlying problems would be necessary to avert violence in the future. Even though we find ourselves in the middle of violence on a massive scale, measures can still be taken to protect the remaining Rohingya in the country who are still at a high risk of future atrocities.

Burma's military is the primary perpetrator of the recent atrocities against Rohingya, aided by a growing number of ethnic Rakhine civilians participating in the attacks as well. Yet, the ultimate responsibility for de-escalating the current cycle of violence and protecting the lives and freedom of Burma's minority populations – from the military as well as non-state groups like ARSA – rests with the country's de facto leader, Aung San Suu Kyi.

As a basic principle, we should not fear pressing democratically elected leaders to squarely confront mass atrocities within their country. We can understand the nature of Burma's democratic transition and the outsized role the military continues to play in national politics, while at the same time expecting moral and uncompromising responses from its civilian-led government. The U.S. Congress does not need to choose between stopping mass atrocities and supporting a democratic government; in Burma, our government can take immediate steps to address the urgent issue of mass atrocities against the Rohingya while laying the groundwork for a democratic future. After all, a democracy in which mass atrocities, even genocide, are occurring is still unacceptable.

In 2012, the United States Holocaust Memorial Museum awarded Aung San Suu Kyi the Elie Wiesel Award, its highest honor, reserved for those prominent individuals whose actions advance the Museum's vision of a world where people confront hatred, prevent genocide, and promote human dignity. Today, these ideals appear absent in the defense of Burma's Rohingya population. We expect her to use her position in government and her even more powerful voice to uphold those very ideals and work to stop the longstanding persecution and violence that threaten the very existence of Rohingya in Burma.

Mr. YOHO. Those were great words. I appreciate that. You know, so many times we promote democracy, and a democracy, if you go back to Ben Franklin, was two wolves and a sheep deciding what to have for lunch. The sheep always loses.

The beauty of our Nation as a republic, a constitutional republic that protects the rights of a minority, and when you have a—you know, I think you said a lot by saying that in the face of fledgling democracy, do we throw everything at that and forsake what is going on on the ground to the people that are getting abused. I appreciate that.

Mr. Lohman, you talked about your five recommendations, and I agree with you. They are good. But I see those as more long-term to prevent future in the future. What do you do for the now, because they need help now? Are they effective enough? If we were to do all five of your recommendations, do you think that would bring the atrocities to an end?

Mr. LOHMAN. No, I don't. I mean, in fact, I agree with you. These are more long-term, broader recommendations getting at the bigger problem, which is the role of the military in Burma and its participation in this sort of thing throughout the country, not just with regard to the Rohingya.

I mean, in my estimation, the most immediate need would be to bring relief to those people now and to end the atrocities and bring relief to them. I mean, unfortunately, we don't have many tools at our disposal, but an effective tool is to actually bring it to an end immediately. I don't think anyone in the U.S. is prepared to bring military force to bear that would do that, and certainly cutting off generals and putting them on the SDN list and that sort of thing, especially since that is going to take a lot of time, it is not going to do it either.

I think the only thing we have right now is moral suasion. We have appeal to the U.N. Security Council. We have some of those things to do, but I don't want to overestimate how much effect that can have on the current situation.

Mr. YOHO. All right. I have a follow-up question. This is going to be to Dr. Martin. The previous U.S. administration dramatically removed U.S. sanctions on Burma following the electoral victory of Aung San Suu Kyi. The National League for Democracy. Was lifting the sanctions a mistake? Should sanctions have been eased in a more gradual stepwise manner, assuming or thinking that in the future sanctions will be put back on?

Mr. MARTIN. Thank you, Mr. Chairman, for the question. As you know, I am an analyst for CRS. In the capacity I am here, I am not supposed to make comment or recommendations.

Mr. YOHO. We won't tell anybody.

Mr. MARTIN. Okay. But I will draw from your previous question in terms of immediate things that can be done. For example, currently, the President has the authority to say for national interest reasons the members of the military can enter the United States, and under JADE Act 5(b), they are not supposed to be given those visas to enter the United States. The administration, both the previous one and the current one, do hand those out with some regularity. So the administration could, at this point, stop handing out those visa waivers. It is immediate action they can take.

Second, section 5(b) of the JADE Act is still in effect in terms of the law. It just has been waived because of the Presidential executive order that said we no longer are going to impose the economic sanctions on four designated categories of people, which includes military leadership. It is within the authority of the President, or whomever he designates, to reverse or undo that executive order. So if you are looking for something that could be done from the administration side revoking that executive order, on doing it would reimpose the SDN list—or excuse me, wouldn't reimpose the SDN list, but would make the JADE Act 5(b) back into effect.

So one of the things that is a little bit complicated in this situation is that many of the laws imposing sanctions are still on the books. They are still there. They are not being enforced right now because of the previous President's waiving of those sanctions.

Mr. YOHO. That is good information, and we will look into doing that immediately and give those recommendations.

Mr. Sullivan, Aung San Suu Kyi has repeatedly stated to the international community, that international coverage of the situation in Rakhine state is biased and inaccurate and incomplete. Is there any merit to her claims? If so, in what respect, and what impact might this have on U.S. relationships with her government? I mean, you have been there.

Mr. SULLIVAN. Yes. Thank you for the question. I think if you are there and you speak to the people about what has happened, it is very clear, as I laid out in my testimony, and this is backed up by satellite images, by videos that have come out. It is very clear that something is happening, so it is honestly mind-boggling that she would say that she doesn't have any idea why, why people are leaving in such numbers. So it can and should have an effect on the bilateral relationship.

Mr. YOHO. Okay. I appreciate your comments. I am out of time.

I am going to yield to the ranking member, Mr. Sherman.

Mr. SHERMAN. Mr. Martin, how much aid do we give to Burma, particularly USAID, do we know?

Mr. MARTIN. I don't know the precise figure off the top of my head. I can certainly——

Mr. SHERMAN. Can you give me a range?

Mr. MARTIN. Roughly about $80 million a year right now, fiscal year.

Mr. SHERMAN. So the first thing we could do is cut back. Is much of that for democracy and human rights promotion or is it mostly economic development?

Mr. MARTIN. There is a combination of economic development/promotion, but also, we have been a significant supporter of the peace process that is underway under the terms of what is called the national ceasefire agreement. Bear in mind, only eight of the roughly 22, 23 EAOs have signed that ceasefire agreement. And I will throw in that——

Mr. SHERMAN. There is the slogan no justice no peace, the idea that we would be giving money to the Burmese Government to help it achieve its objectives. Now, human rights and democracy may not be its objectives, but anything that is consistent that we would be giving them money for that seems absurd, especially when we are talking about doing things that would cost the U.S. taxpayer money, such as sanctions or humanitarian aid, all of which may be warranted, but we should first do the thing that reduces expenditures.

I am going to ask this question probably for the record, unless somebody knows, but I hope Dr. Martin and his team at the CRS will get me an answer. What is being done to publicize to the Muslim world China's support for this murderous regime? And what is being done to publicize the fact that we are doing more to protect the Rohingya than any other state, other than those in the immediate neighborhood?

I don't see anyone anxious to answer that question right now, so I will ask that for the record.

Now, an uncomfortable question: Is ARSA engaging in some smaller atrocities? And given our support for the Rohingya, can we persuade them to limit their actions to those against the Burmese military?

Mr. Lohman, or anyone else?

Mr. SULLIVAN. There are reports of ARSA carrying out attacks and——

Mr. SHERMAN. Against civilians?

Mr. SULLIVAN. Yes. And, of course——

Mr. SHERMAN. And for the record, they are tiny in quantity compared to what the Rohingya people are facing. At the same time, they undermine the moral case that we are trying to make. They also undermine the ability of the Burmese Government to change its policy and become more reasonable. One atrocity against Buddhists in Rakhine State could make it difficult for those inside the Burmese Government to change its policy.

Let's see. Is Voice of America carrying the message that it should? Does the average person in Burma know what the world thinks of what their government is doing?

Mr. Lohman? Anybody know? If we don't have an answer, I will ask for the record.

Mr. MARTIN. I can get you more information, sir. I know Radio Free Asia, for example, has regular stories about what is going on in Rakhine State.

Mr. SHERMAN. And are those in——

Mr. MARTIN. They focus primarily——

Mr. SHERMAN. Are those in the Burmese language?

Mr. MARTIN. Yes, there is a Voice of America-Radio Free Asia Burmese broadcast.

Mr. SHERMAN. One would hope that they would have the courage at the Burmese service to push these stories, not just in the—I assume we have a—that we also broadcast in the language of Bangladesh. It is a lot easier for that service to cover this message.

I will just throw this out here: If the Burmese Government disenfranchises some of its people—I mean, a government has a certain amount of territory for the benefit of its people. They have disclaimed over 1 million of their people. If they permanently show that they are unwilling or unable to protect the Rohingya, is a long-term solution the transfer of territory to Bangladesh?

We obviously, as a Nation, don't like to see sovereign borders change, but when a nation refuses to allow its own people to live on its territory, it loses the right to control that territory.

Dr.Martin?

Mr. MARTIN. Real quick. Since you bring that up, because in the early days when there was a previous insurgent group among the Rohingya, what they wanted at that time was to be part of what was Pakistan, East Pakistan.

Mr. SHERMAN. Which is today Bangladesh.

Mr. MARTIN. Which is today Bangladesh.

So I do not know if Aung San's leadership or the Rohingya people in general would want that——

Mr. SHERMAN. Obviously, the first choice is the return of the refugees' citizenship, protection, and living in harmony with the other people of Rakhine State. But if that cannot be achieved, then a transfer of population has been achieved through this ethnic cleansing; perhaps a transfer of territory would go along with it.

For the record, I want to point out that the Ambassador for Bangladesh has no comment.

Mr. YOHO. Thank you, Mr. Chairman.

We will now go to Mrs. Ann Wagner.

Mrs. WAGNER. Thank you, Mr. Chairman, very, very much. I appreciate it, as I said in my opening statement, your willingness to hold this hearing.

In 2013, there was an article in the Emory International Law Review calling for an international investigation into mass atrocity crimes against Rohingya Muslims. I know this because one of my staff members, Rachel Wagley, actually published the article.

Sadly, everything written then is just as pertinent today, and this was back in 2013. It is heartbreaking how little the conflict has changed.

Ms. Gittleman, you wrote that even if an investigation is conducted, we cannot wait for a formal finding of genocide to take action. I agree.

What are the obstacles to establishing an international investigation? Where is the United Nations? And how do you believe the U.S. should leverage its influence to spur some sort of international investigation?

Ms. GITTLEMAN. Well, thank you for the question, Representative Wagner.

I think this is a really important issue. The reason why we might not have sufficient information in order to make a legal declaration about the situation is because it is so difficult to access the areas of northern Rakhine State where the military has been committing these crimes. There has been a fact-finding mission that was created by the United Nations Human Rights Council.

So far, the Burmese Government has resisted any efforts to cooperate with that mission to allow them to undertake their investigation in a way that would get them the access that they require. I think the situation now in the face of denials and obstacles placed by the Burmese Government that requires a greater push internationally for an independent investigation.

I think the United States is well placed as one of the key players, both on the Security Council and as one of the forces that I think would help mobilize more support for an international investigation.

This would be an extremely important next step.

Mrs. WAGNER. It has been going on, well, for 60 years, but for 5 years now with Rohingya Muslims. Well past time.

Ms. Gittleman or Mr. Sullivan, we hear so many stories of rape and sexual abuse coming out of Burma, and you outlined some of that, Ms. Gittleman. The Bangladesh Embassy has reported that many of the Rohingya flowing into Bangladesh are women and children.

Can you talk about the risks facing women and girls in Rakhine State and help us understand how the international humanitarian response can better confront sexual violence?

Ms. GITTLEMAN. Sure, I will address quickly and then turn to my colleague.

What we have seen from people who have fled such horrific violence and who have come into Bangladesh, many have shared stories of use of rape and other forms of sexual violence. The way that they describe these crimes being committed makes it appear that they are being done systematically so that it is being used as a weapon specifically against women and girls, against Rohingya women and girls. This is not ad hoc. This isn't something extraneous. It certainly isn't part of any kind of counterinsurgency operation.

This is something that has been—we have heard stories from people from across different geographic areas, which leads us to believe this might be something that is quite widespread.

So, if you imagine women and girls fleeing from their homes, seeing horrific violence, being subjected to sexual violence, running, getting over the border, which may take days or weeks, once they arrive with very little possessions, little money, then they need to set about accessing the kind of healthcare and services that they would require. And you can only imagine how daunting that must be for people who have experienced so much trauma. So there needs to be assistance to make sure that those many people can get the aid that they need.

Mrs. WAGNER. Let me just jump in here because I have limited time, as I have another question that I want to—thank you very much. It is just horrific.

I am so disappointed and angered, frankly, by Suu Kyi's actions or lack of actions. To whoever can best answer, has she made some sort of agreement with the Burmese military to enable violence against Rohingya? Does she have any political room whatsoever to provide any moral leadership at this point with respect to the Rohingya? Surely other minorities in the country can sympathize with the plight of the Rohingya. Please.

Mr. SULLIVAN. Yeah, I can't speculate as to what her motivations are, and I share the disappointment. But the fact is she does have a powerful voice and she was voted in overwhelming, has lots of support that she can garner.

Just quickly on your previous question, I would just point to, as I mentioned in my testimony, I was in Bangladesh a few months ago, and Refugees International released a report at that time in July based on what had happened since the influx of 87,000 Rohingya after October 2016 and talked about the gender-based violence and the accounts that we heard. So you can only imagine that today, with over 400,000——

Mrs. WAGNER. Right.

Mr. SULLIVAN [continuing]. Approaching 500,000 now, what level of a challenge that is. And there were doctors from the U.N. just yesterday or the day before who came out and talked about documenting dozens of cases.

Mrs. WAGNER. Thank you.

Thank you, Mr. Chairman. I yield back.

Mr. YOHO. Thank you, Ms. Wagner.

We will now go to Dr. Bera from California.

Mr. BERA. Thank you, Mr. Chairman.

Thank you to the ranking member, and also thank you to the witnesses.

You know, this is tragic. I mean, as Mr. Sullivan pointed out, we are seeing genocide and ethnic cleansing repeating itself. If we just think about our moral character and our values as a Nation, we can't sit idly by. You have outlined a few ways that we can approach this in terms of trying to leverage the Burmese Government and the Burmese military.

From the public perspective, in my own community back in Sacramento, different groups are starting to come back, religious groups, public advocates, et cetera. They are trying to raise awareness. So, again, a lot of people aren't paying attention to the plight of the Rohingya, but they are trying to raise local awareness.

Mr. Sullivan, maybe from your perspective, what can the public do right now because we also want to see that public pressure?

Mr. SULLIVAN. Yes. Thank you. I think going back to what you do in democracy, you contact your representatives, and hopefully there are more like those on this subcommittee that are hearing about this and speaking out and realizing how urgent of a situation this is. As I mentioned, it is just patently different from pretty much anything I have ever seen. It is just really urgent. I think there are a lot of advocacy groups out there that try to get this information out and get people motivated.

Mr. BERA. So just trying to raise the volume on it——

Mr. SULLIVAN. Raise the volume——

Mr. BERA [continuing]. So more and more people are aware——

Mr. SULLIVAN [continuing]. Reach out to local newspapers that kind of thing.

Mr. BERA. Maybe sticking with you, Mr. Sullivan, I am a physician by training with a background in public health. Thinking about the number of refugees who have fled to Bangladesh, you mentioned that you were recently in the camps there. Can you talk about the conditions in the camp?

Mr. SULLIVAN. Sure. As I say, it was just starkly different from just a few months ago where areas that had been all green are just overrun. People carrying bamboo sticks and tarps and rope to try to prop up shelters. The monsoon rains are going on, so people walking through ankle-deep mud. It is just an immense challenge just to record who is coming in.

The Bangladesh Government, working with UNHCR and others have begun to take biometric information and give out cards to try to keep track of who is there. But they have maybe done around 13,000 of the nearing 500,000 that are there now.

Mr. BERA. Okay. The majority are in camps, and what we have seen in Jordan with Syrian refugees is they have tried to assimilate them and get them into urban communities. But I have to imagine the majority in Bangladesh are living in camp-like settings. That raises public health concerns, and real public health concerns because not just the tragedy of being forced from their home; now we very much have to think about the possibilities of disease and so forth and the toll that would take on morbidity.

Are they seeing those public health issues right now?

Mr. SULLIVAN. Yes, it is a huge risk. I mean, there was already, there were outbreaks after the October influx. This is just on a much larger scale. So, yeah, it is a very high risk.

Mr. BERA. Bangladesh is not a wealthy country. What can and what should we be doing at the congressional level and at the international level to help support the refugees?

Mr. SULLIVAN. As I mentioned, there was $32 million that the U.S. Government gave, but the needs are a lot more. So getting that financial support out there and making sure that there is proper coordination and going along with guidelines, internationally accepted guidelines, building shelters, and providing medical care.

Mr. BERA. My colleague, Mr. Sherman, has identified $80 million that potentially we could move over.

You know, it is tragic. I know we can't speculate on Aung San Suu Kyi's motives here, but for someone who has previously been held in pretty high regard by many of us, the lack of not using that bully pulpit to speak out and push back—I mean, this is a person who previously has shown moral courage. If they are paying attention and listening, if she is watching this, there was never a time for moral courage like the time right now.

So this is the time to use that bully pulpit.

Thank you, and I will yield back.

Mr. YOHO. Thank you, Dr. Bera.

Now, we will go to Mr. Rohrabacher from California.

Mr. ROHRABACHER. Thank you very much, Mr. Chairman. Just a suggestion, and first of all, I appreciate your holding this conference. I have learned a lot. That is the purpose of the conference. We would have learned more, I believe, had we had someone from the Burmese Government here to give their side of the story.

I have been chairman of various subcommittees. No matter how reprehensible the other side is on whatever issue, I have always made sure that both sides had a chance. I think it would have been interesting to hear an interaction and charges and refutations and how someone would have responded to the charges we have heard today.

I have learned a lot, as I say. Let me ask some more fundamental questions here. In the Rakhine State, how many of those people are Rohingyas—I am sorry I mispronounced it—what percentage are that, and what percentage are other ethnic groups?

Mr. MARTIN. Congressman Rohrabacher, let me try to give you a rough idea. First off, the easiest answer is no one actually knows. A couple years ago, Burma tried to conduct a nationwide census of its population, the first one in decades. But when it came to Rakhine State, when they wanted to do a census of the Rohingya households, the provision was they had to self-identify as Bengalis. That was objectionable to all those——

Mr. ROHRABACHER. What is your guess as to——

Mr. MARTIN. Well, the figure that is normally put around is 1 million to 1.1 million Rohingya.

Mr. ROHRABACHER. Okay. And the population of——

Mr. MARTIN. And then I can't remember the exact figure off the top of my head of the Rakhine. The Rakhine, who tend to live in the southern part of the state, are the majority of the population, but scattered throughout the state are other ethnic groups. Interestingly enough, there is another group called the Kamar, who are also Sunni Muslims.

Mr. ROHRABACHER. Okay.

Mr. MARTIN. They are citizens——

Mr. ROHRABACHER. Okay.

Mr. MARTIN [continuing]. But they are a very small percentage. Then you have——

Mr. ROHRABACHER. So, overall, what is the guess of the population?

Mr. MARTIN. I believe the figure is around 5 million.

Mr. ROHRABACHER. Two million? Five million?

Mr. MARTIN. Yeah, I would have to double check that on you.

Mr. ROHRABACHER. Okay. We don't know.

Okay. Anybody else have a guess?

Okay. I don't want to even guess, but there are 1 million people that are part of this ethnic group that now has been targeted. We know that. And they were denied citizenship. This ethnic group that we are talking about today has been present in this state since Burma became a country in 1948. This is not a new group that showed up.

So to claim that they are illegal immigrants, which Burma does, is inaccurate in that they have been there the whole time.

Let me just note, in Burma, having a little background in Burma, I know about the Chins, the Kachin, the Karens, the Karennis. And now we know this ethnic group as well as—they are in the same area. There are several ethnic groups.

So the idea that if there is ever going to be any peace in that country, basically the Burmese who control the capital and control the country as a whole, had better be accepting of that or there is just going to be one big blood bath as we have seen, by the way. There were, again, hundreds of thousands of Karens and Karenni who were Christians, who had to leave Burma in order to flee for Thailand, 20, 30 years ago. I know I visited them and I visited Aung San Suu Kyi when she was under house arrest. And let me just say I, too, am disappointed that she has not spoken up.

Only a respect for human rights by that country as a whole with all of these people is going to bring about, you know, any type of peace or an end to this.

Let me just note that there—and thank you very much for the good job you did with the Congressional Research Service on giving us a background. I notice that the militant group that is supportive of, and again, the Rohingyas, actually, in August 2017, conducted a coordinated attack on 30 police and army outposts. So this isn't a bunch of passifists who are now being slaughtered by the Burmese military.

On October 2016, there was, again, attacks by this particular, the army representing this ethnic group. I think if we are going to be peacemakers in the world, which I think the United States should be—and I agree with you that we need to participate, go down there and participate in an international investigation. But we need to be really honest about what we see and not, again, just take sides because you will get a headline for today, or it seems that this is what the reality is, even though we haven't investigated it.

So this reminds me a lot, Mr. Chairman, of the—pardon me for talking too long here—reminds me of another crisis we went through early on between the Serbs and the Kosovars. It reminds me a lot of that. The Serbs were involved with all kinds of violent activity, and the Burmese remind me a lot of the Serbs at their worst.

But let me just say that we should be a force for good in this world and to find out truth. And with truth, we do need both sides to be telling us their story. And I would hope that someday that we can play a positive role with the Burmese.

With that said, thank you very much for your testimony. I have learned a lot.

I will be looking forward to working with you, Mr. Chairman, to make sure that we play a positive role.

One last question. How much have our Muslim friends in other countries, especially oil-rich countries, contributed to the plight of these poor people who are now being pushed into Bangladesh and are under such horrible circumstances?

Has there been any major help being offered by their fellow Muslims? Do we know?

Mr. MARTIN. Yes. Saudi Arabia, in particular, has been outspoken, as has Malaysia recently, in terms of seeking support for this community. And I can't think of the name right now, but one of the multilateral Islamic groups has tried to go into Rakhine State to provide assistance in the past but has been rebuffed by the government.

Mr. ROHRABACHER. Rebuffed by the Bangladesh Government?

Mr. MARTIN. No, this is inside Burma.

Mr. ROHRABACHER. Oh, inside Burma.

Mr. MARTIN. Inside Myanmar.

Mr. ROHRABACHER. Okay. Well, I am not looking for people who are outspoken. I am looking for someone who is outspent. So I hope we could get some assistance down, because what was described today, these people are in a desperate situation. Good people around the world should try to save them in this desperate situation.

Thank you very much, Mr. Chairman.

Mr. YOHO. Thank you both for your comments.

We will next go to Mr. Connolly from Virginia.

Mr. CONNOLLY. Thank you, Mr. Chairman.

And welcome to our panel.

Mr. Sullivan—well, any of you—I mean, is this, from an international legal point of view, ethnic cleansing?

Mr. SULLIVAN. Ethnic cleansing doesn't have a clear, legal definition, but by any kind of standards of what it has been described of as displacing an entire group of people forcibly, then yes, it absolutely—and as the High Commissioner for Human Rights has said, it is a textbook case of ethnic cleansing.

Mr. CONNOLLY. Right. So you are right: It is not exactly a legal concept, I suppose, in the Hague, but when the Commissioner for Human Rights uses it, it has some force of meaning.

Do we believe that it is the intention of the Burmese Government or Burmese military, or both to, in fact, cleanse Burma of the Rohingya, period?

Any of you can feel free.

Ms. GITTLEMAN. There are many legal terms that can be used to describe this situation. Crimes against humanity appears——

Mr. CONNOLLY. No, no. Ms. Gittleman, my question is: Do we believe that it is the intention of the military or the Government of Burma to, in fact, eliminate the Rohingya from Burma or Myanmar?

Ms. GITTLEMAN. What we are seeing today is a campaign of ethnic cleansing. What we don't know——

Mr. CONNOLLY. Ms. Gittleman, I know that.

Ms. GITTLEMAN.—is the exact intent——

Mr. CONNOLLY. We have established that. I am asking a different question.

Is it the intention, do we believe, of the current Government or the military of Myanmar to essentially be Rohingya-free? Is that what they are doing?

Ms. GITTLEMAN. What we don't know is the exact intent of those perpetrators?

Mr. CONNOLLY. Mr. Lohman, do you have any views on that matter?

Mr. LOHMAN. No, I mean, I agree. We don't——

Mr. CONNOLLY. Please speak into the microphone, Mr. Lohman.

Mr. LOHMAN. We don't know their intent. I mean, how can we know their intent?

Mr. CONNOLLY. Can you make a wild guess given the fact that ¾ of 1 million people are in Bangladesh?

Mr. LOHMAN. Yes, absolutely. I would say, by the looks of it, yes, it is ethnic cleansing.

Mr. CONNOLLY. Dr.Martin? No, I am not asking that question.

Mr. LOHMAN. Okay.

Mr. CONNOLLY. Are they trying to make sure that Burma or Myanmar is in fact free of all Rohingyas? Is that their goal? So that that ethnic minority no longer is present in their country? That is my question.

Is there a strategic goal here, besides, "We just don't like them, and we are responding," as you in your testimony said, clearly overreacting, "to insurgent attacks on the Burmese military"?

Mr. MARTIN. I will speak to the record of what we know from what has been said. Aung San Suu Kyi in her speech of September 19 to the international community said that she would welcome the return of the Rohingya. However, it is under a 1993 agreement with Bangladesh and its provisions about documentation or verification of the fact that they were residents, not necessarily citizens, of Burma before.

So I believe there is some indication, at least on her statements, of a willingness to see a return of some portion, exactly what portion, of the roughly ½ million who have left.

Mr. CONNOLLY. But she——

Mr. MARTIN. Now, in terms of the military, I did speak to a lieutenant general when I was in Naypyitaw just 2 weeks ago. They do not portray this as any effort on their part to try to make the people move out of the area. All they are doing is pursuing ARSA's members and their sympathizers.

However, I cannot find the quote right now, but there was a quote from a few years ago when there was a similar incidence of Rohingya leaving, where somebody senior in the military said, "If some friendly nation will take all 1 million of them, we would be happy to see them all leave."

Mr. CONNOLLY. Yeah.

Mr. MARTIN. And that is on the historical record. So I would suspect one could infer that, at least in the Tatmadaw, there are some who would——

Mr. CONNOLLY. Thank you.

Mr. MARTIN [continuing]. Welcome it.

Mr. CONNOLLY. Thank you. Because I think we have to be clear about that. I mean, frankly futzing around about, "Well, we are not sure about their intent, who can read their minds," their behavior is what tells us what is happening. This isn't some localized action. This is mass relocation of people to another country. And thank God Bangladesh is there and willing to accept them. I mean, the international community owes Bangladesh, a very poor country, a great debt of gratitude for receiving the Rohingya, it seems to me. They are a poor country. They already had large numbers of the Rohingya already there, and now they are almost doubling, more than doubling that population.

Have people in, besides Aung San Suu Kyi, have people in the legislative body in Myanmar spoken out against what is happening? Anyone know?

Mr. SULLIVAN. I haven't seen any speaking out within the Parliament. The popular opinion is very much against the Rohingya and——

Mr. CONNOLLY. Right.

Mr. SULLIVAN [continuing]. It is a very dangerous kind of thing to speak out, which is why the international pressure is so much more important.

Mr. CONNOLLY. And, Dr. Martin, I think you cited the Aung San Suu Kyi, but she is severely circumscribed by the military. I mean, she doesn't control the military directly. So, if the military wants to continue doing this, it is not entirely within her ability to influence that situation.

I was in—I am sorry—Myanmar, last year, and I was very struck by the competing centers of power in Naypyitaw and the great caution with which each side sort of wanders past the other.

Mr. Lohman, you look like you wanted to comment on that. I would welcome the comment.

Mr. LOHMAN. I was going to say, I mean, I agree with that sentiment. And I——

Mr. CONNOLLY. Please speak into the microphone.

Mr. LOHMAN [continuing]. I may be in the minority here, but I
think we have to be careful not to be too hard on Aung San Suu
Kyi as I do think she is very tightly restrained.

Mr. CONNOLLY. Right.

Mr. LOHMAN. I find it hard to believe that in the last 20 years,
she has completely changed her character to the point where she
would support this kind of thing.

If anything, I think her remarks are a demonstration of how
tightly constrained she is.

Mr. CONNOLLY. Yeah.

Mr. LOHMAN. She could come out tomorrow and be very vocal
about it, but how is that going to change the situation? That
doesn't pull on the heartstrings of the military. They could care
less what she thinks or anybody else in the civilian government
thinks.

They could end this whole experiment in democracy tomorrow if
they want, and I think she well understands that. So I don't want
to give her a complete benefit of the doubt. I know she said some
things that are a little bit puzzling and disturbing, sort of in a positive sense. She said things about Rohingya that make you wonder.
But I think we do have to give her a little bit of the benefit of a
doubt. We haven't supported her for 25 years for nothing.

Mr. CONNOLLY. I am going to end, Mr. Chairman, but I just
think that is a very critical point. I thank Mr. Lohman for making
that point.

I was struck by the same thing. The latitude she has, especially
when the military is involved, is very limited. It is a very delicate
dance with two powers coexisting very uneasily in Myanmar. None
of that is to say one should not speak out about a blatant human
rights violation such as we are witnessing now. But as to her intent and how she is reacting, there are some severe limitations on
her that could have severe consequences if she stepped over un-
written boundaries.

So we do need to understand that as we approach this massive
human rights problem.

Thank you, Mr. Chairman.

Mr. YOHO. I appreciate your input. We will next go to Mr. Perry
from Pennsylvania.

Mr. PERRY. Thank you, Mr. Chairman, ladies and gentlemen on
the panel.

How many Rohingya are left? What is the estimate? Is there 1
million to start or do we know?

Mr. MARTIN. Like I said earlier, there is no accurate figures on
exactly how many were there beforehand. But if we say roughly ½
million have fled at this point since August——

Mr. PERRY. August 25th, accordingto this.

Mr. MARTIN. August 25th, that would reduce that population to
half. You had 87,000 before, earlier in the year. So roughly somewhere between a quarter to half.

Mr. PERRY. Quarter to half a million left, right?

Mr. MARTIN. Of the percentage; 200,000 to 500,000.

Mr. PERRY. 200,000 to 500,000. And according to this, this is what I referenced. I read it last night. Wall Street Journal article from a week or so ago: Since August 25th, an estimated 430,000 have fled Rakhine State.

So, if the numbers are accurate here, in about a month, I mean, we are all talking here, right? These people are being—heck, if they are lucky, they are being kicked out. If they are unlucky, they are not going to make it anywhere. They are dying in place. That is what it seems to me. It seems like it was about a month ago.

So my question is, what can be done right now? How is an investigation going to happen in a sovereign nation that refuses to let anybody come in to investigate?

Ms. GITTLEMAN. Well, I think you raise an important question about all the Rohingya who remain in northern Rakhine State. We know the numbers of people who have crossed to Bangladesh, but there remains a significant fraction who are still in northern Rakhine State, whether they are displaced from their homes we don't know because we can't access the area. But those people, of course, remain at extremely high risk of atrocities, if they haven't been targeted yet.

Mr. PERRY. Yeah, I imagine.

Ms. GITTLEMAN. So they would require protection. They require aid, just as people who have crossed the border have.

Mr. PERRY. So no sooner is Burma or Myanmar, or whatever you want to call it, going to allow, as a sovereign nation, going to allow the United States or Bangladesh or China or anybody else come in and tell them how to run their railroad; the answer seems to be somewhere in the U.N., right?

The clock is ticking. So, since we are not probably going to be able to force anything as a sovereign nation, any more than we would want Burma to force anything on the United States, what is the United Nations doing, and what are we doing in concert with the United Nations right now to take action right now, today, within a few days? Because in 30 days, we probably won't talk about this anymore because it will be history, right? We will be writing about it. So what is happening now?

Mr. SULLIVAN. Yeah, tomorrow, the U.N. Secretary General will be addressing the U.N. Security Council for the first time in open debate. There has been closed discussion.

It was very welcome that the Trump administration, after about 3 weeks, came out with a call for the U.N. Security Council to take swift action.

I would say that, you know, I laid out some of the things I would recommend, including the multilateral sanctions, arms embargo.

On the accountability——

Mr. PERRY. Sir, with all due respect, I don't think the U.N. needed to wait for President Trump to come out. This is what we have a U.N. for. Talking about sanctions when this is going to be over in a month, according to these numbers, or substantially if these hold, a discussion tomorrow is meaningless. What you need is a vote. And Burma has to accept some kind of envoy to go into their country and witness and have an investigation. Everybody in the room knows it. Other than that, all we are talking about is platitudes and we wish this could happen.

Sanctions aren't going to do anything in that amount of time. By the time sanctions matter, it is all going to be over. And they are not even having the discussion yet.

Mr. SULLIVAN. Well, I agree. But I think you can't wait for that. And there are things that are being done. Like the U.N. fact-finding mission is going to Bangladesh, where they can access people, and collecting evidence.

Mr. PERRY. Are they going to be allowed to be in Rakhine State, this fact-finding mission?

Mr. SULLIVAN. The government has said they will not allow them.

Mr. PERRY. So all that is pointless as well.

While I appreciate the information, I appreciate your passion, compassion, and your interest in this, it is very frustrating. But all we are doing is talking right now, and it doesn't seem like there is a solution in this room that is recognized. The solution is at the U.N.

And somebody ought to not wait until tomorrow. Somebody ought to be meeting right now and not having a discussion about, "Is this happening," but have a vote right now tonight, today, on going in there and doing something, right? That is what needs to happen. Otherwise, this is all just unfortunate conjecture, and these poor people are either going to leave or be killed. That is the answer, unfortunately.

Mr. Chairman, I yield.

Mr. YOHO. I appreciate your comments and your passion. And you bring up a very good point.

Mr. Sullivan, reading your—I believe it is your testimony. Yeah, it was yours—your recommendations, "Congress should," and you listed several things: Press the Trump administration to work through the U.N. Security Council.

One of your bulleted points were support for a referral to the International Criminal Court unless Myanmar authorities take significant measures to address the human rights.

I am thinking the same thing Mr. Perry did. Why?

I mean, we see what is going on. We need to put the pressure on now. Our recommendations that are going to come out of this meeting because of you guys are going to be for JADE Act to be revoked immediately. The $63 million that was requested for aid to Burma, our recommendation is we are going to hold that. Our team doesn't know that yet. I guess they do now. Then to go to the U.N. and say, "you need to do something now. We demand you act now."

This is something, again, that we are in the 21st century, and I see these atrocities going on that makes you not even want to be part of the human race to see these going on. Everybody out here, in here, has a Representative that you vote for. Demand that they do something about that. Please do something about that.

Let's see, what else do I have here? This is a question I want to ask. If you all can comment on this, if you have time for one more question: Burma is a member of the ASEAN nations, one of the members of 10 nations. What is the sentiment of the other nations in ASEAN with this kind of action? Do they have the wherewithal, the fortitude to say, "What you are doing is wrong, and you need to bring it to an end"?

What are your thoughts on that? We will start with Dr. Martin, if you have time and patience.

Mr. MARTIN. Sure. Real quickly. ASEAN actually just recently released a statement with respect to what is going on in Burma, or Myanmar, as they call it. It was expressing concern, would be the way I would phrase it. Malaysia objected to that statement saying that it did not address sufficiently the situation in Rakhine State or the situation for the Rohingya.

Two other aspects with respect to ASEAN: They have a traditional policy of noninterference in internal affairs, and so this would be considered possibly an internal affair; they don't want to get involved. However, they also have set up an ASEAN Human Rights Commission, which has been criticized for being ineffective and not taking much action. So one could argue that this is a time where the ASEAN Human Rights Commission could step up and take an active interest.

Mr. YOHO. Mr. Lohman?

Mr. LOHMAN. Yeah, if you think the U.N. is ineffective addressing the situation, ASEAN is completely useless.

So, I mean, because of their noninterference principle and other considerations, you know, they have watched this over the last 25 years or so and done really nothing about the whole range of issues in Burma.

So I wouldn't expect much, at least in being able to help this current situation.

The one area that might be able to be of some assistance is helping to get humanitarian aid into the country. Back in 2008, they played a role in cyclone. In August, I was there and they did play a role; it was very late. The Burmese prevented humanitarian assistance from coming in to address the results of a natural disaster, but eventually they did, and they did through ASEAN. So they may be able to be of some help in that regard.

Mr. SULLIVAN. I would just add that the Prime Minister of Thailand will be meeting with the White House early next week. So that is an opportunity to express their need to put more pressure on Myanmar and to accept Rohingya who are fleeing.

Ms. GITTLEMAN. I think we are seeing growing concern from other countries in the region, which as I said, is a different tack. With ASEAN, of course, they have been premised on cooperation, and I think it is the sheer urgency of this crisis that is making some countries in the region change their tune.

Mr. YOHO. I just want to say how much I appreciate you all being here because you are bringing to light, you know, you are shining a light on just a terrible tragedy and atrocity that is going on around the world.

As you brought up, Mr. Sullivan, how many times are we going to go through this? We have seen this throughout history. We have seen it, you know, Auschwitz, in World War II and all the genocide that happened there. Rwanda, Bosnia, Serbia, Darfur.

How many more times do we want to tolerate this? There has got to be a better way. The U.N. is an effective—but there needs to be an enforcement mechanism within the U.N., a multinational enforcement, that can bring this kind of garbage to an end. These kinds of crimes against humanity just need to be brought to an end. And the people that are responsible for this, we need to prosecute those people, and it needs to be done rapidly to send a signal out to the rest of the world.

And for clarification, it was not a very revocation of the JADE Act. It was the no waiver on the—I can't read that—what does that say—on the sanctions.

So we are going to act on what you guys told us. I appreciate it.

Ambassador Ziauddin, thank you for being here and what your country is doing. Our office is going to reach out to you to work on this more specifically.

With that, the meeting is adjourned.

The notes will be added to the congressional record, and we thank you again for your time, your patience, and your tolerance.

[Whereupon, at 4:09 p.m., the subcommittee was adjourned.]

A P P E N D I X

―――――

Material Submitted for the Record

SUBCOMMITTEE HEARING NOTICE
COMMITTEE ON FOREIGN AFFAIRS
U.S. HOUSE OF REPRESENTATIVES
WASHINGTON, DC 20515-6128

Subcommittee on Asia and the Pacific
Ted Yoho (R-FL), Chairman

September 27, 2017

TO: MEMBERS OF THE COMMITTEE ON FOREIGN AFFAIRS

You are respectfully requested to attend an OPEN hearing of the Committee on Foreign Affairs, to be held by the Subcommittee on Asia and the Pacific in Room 2172 of the Rayburn House Office Building (and available live on the Committee website at http://www.ForeignAffairs.house.gov):

DATE: Wednesday, September 27, 2017

TIME: 2:30 p.m.

SUBJECT: Burma's Brutal Campaign Against the Rohingya

WITNESSES: Mr. Walter Lohman
Director
Asian Studies Center
Davis Institute for National Security and Foreign Policy
The Heritage Foundation

Mr. Daniel P. Sullivan
Senior Advocate for Human Rights
Refugees International

Michael F. Martin, Ph.D.
Specialist in Asian Affairs
Foreign Affairs, Defense, and Trade Division
Congressional Research Service

Ms. Andrea Gittleman
Program Manager
Simon-Skjodt Center for the Prevention of Genocide
U.S. Holocaust Memorial Museum

By Direction of the Chairman

The Committee on Foreign Affairs seeks to make its facilities accessible to persons with disabilities. If you are in need of special accommodations, please call 202/225-5021 at least four business days in advance of the event, whenever practicable. Questions with regard to special accommodations in general (including availability of Committee materials in alternative formats and assistive listening devices) may be directed to the Committee.

COMMITTEE ON FOREIGN AFFAIRS

MINUTES OF SUBCOMMITTEE ON _______________ *Asia and the Pacific* _______________ HEARING

Day __*Wednesday*__ Date ____*9/27/2017*____ Room ___*RHOB 2172*___

Starting Time ___*3:34 pm*___ Ending Time __*4:10 pm*___

Recesses |____| (____to ____) (____to ____) (____to ____) (____to ____) (____to ____) (____to ____)

Presiding Member(s)

Chairman Ted Yoho

Check all of the following that apply:

Open Session ☑ Electronically Recorded (taped) ☐
Executive (closed) Session ☐ Stenographic Record ☐
Televised ☐

TITLE OF HEARING:

"Burma's Brutal Campaign Against the Rohingya"

SUBCOMMITTEE MEMBERS PRESENT:

*Rep. Ted Yoho, Rep. Ann Wagner, Rep. Dana Rohrabacher, Rep. Scott Perry, Rep. Steve Chabot
Rep. Brad Sherman, Rep. Ami Bera, Rep. Gerald Connolly*

NON-SUBCOMMITTEE MEMBERS PRESENT: *(Mark with an * if they are not members of full committee.)*

Rep. Ed Royce

HEARING WITNESSES: Same as meeting notice attached? Yes ☑ **No** ☐
(If "no", please list below and include title, agency, department, or organization.)

STATEMENTS FOR THE RECORD: *(List any statements submitted for the record.)*

Connolly SFR

TIME SCHEDULED TO RECONVENE __________
or
TIME ADJOURNED __________

____
Subcommittee Staff Associate

<u>**Statement for the Record**</u>
Rep. Gerald Connolly
AP Subcommittee Hearing: "Burma's Brutal Campaign Against the Rohingya"
September 27, 2017

On August 25, Rohingya militants attacked around 30 police and army outposts, leaving 12 Burmese officers dead. Following these attacks, the Burmese military has embarked on a violent retaliation campaign, including razing Rohingya villages, placing landmines along the border, killing civilians, and committing sexual violence. While the Burmese military claims that this campaign is a "clearance operation" against an insurgent terrorist group, their actions targeting civilians tell a different and abhorrent story. The United Nations High Commissioner for Human Rights Zeid Ra'ad al-Hussein has called these atrocities a "textbook example of ethnic cleansing."

Tragically, state-sponsored persecution and violence against the Rohingya in Burma is nothing new. In 2014, I joined several of my colleagues in writing to the Administration to outline a few disturbing trends in Burma's democratic transition, including continued discrimination and violence against the Rohingya. The latest violent crackdown has only compounded such concerns. Last year, I visited Burma with the House Democracy Partnership to meet with members of the legislature and the new democratically elected government of Aung San Suu Kui. The United States needs to strike a balance between supporting Burma's democratic transition, while urging an end to violence and discrimination against Rohingya. The outsize power of the military within Burma's civilian government is an obstacle to Burma's democratic progress and hinders the government's attempts to prevent an explosion of sectarian violence in Rakhine State. Burma's government must cease its policy of keeping the minority Rohingya population stateless, displaced, and in a constant state of humanitarian crisis.

The recent wave of violence in Burma's northern Rakhine State has sparked the region's largest refugee crisis ever, and the world's fastest growing humanitarian crisis. An estimated 480,000 refugees and counting have fled to Bangladesh. The sheer volume has quickly overwhelmed Bangladesh's two formal refugee camps, and the vast majority of refugees are now living in fragile and unsanitary conditions in informal camps, roadside settlements, and even in uninhabited forest. Bangladesh has shown incredible generosity in welcoming these refugees, especially given that 350,000 Rohingya refugees were already in the country prior to this latest crisis.

Lack of clean water, poor hygene conditions, and acute shortages of food and medicine could lead to a full-blown health crisis. The Bangladesh authorities have already reported thousands of cases of diarrhea, respiratory problems, and skin diseases, and the World Health Organization has warned of a growing risk of a cholera epidemic. I urge the Bangladesh Government to lift existing restrictions on international non-governmental organizations so that a coordinated global effort can stave off a health emergency.

During the 72nd Session of the United Nations General Assembly last week, the United States announced an additional $32 million in humanitarian assistance for Rohingya internally displaced in Rakhine State and the refugees and host communities in Bangladesh. This supplemental provision brings total U.S. humanitarian assistance for Rohingya to nearly $95 million in FY 2017. Nonetheless, the U.N. High Commissioner for Refugees has called for a redoubling of the international humanitarian response in Bangladesh, citing the pace and extreme vulnerability of refugees.

The Rohingya are one of the most persecuted communities around the world. They have endured horrific abuses at the hand of the Burmese Government for far too long. As Bangladesh prepares to host more than one million Rohingya refugees, the international community must band together to address both the urgent humanitarian needs and the long-term societal needs of the Rohingya people. I look forward to hearing from our witnesses on how Congress can continue to assist in both of these respects.